Also by Patrick Barry

Good with Words: Writing and Editing

THE Syntax OF Sports

Class 1: The Words under the Words

Patrick Barry

Published in the United States of America by
Michigan Publishing
Manufactured in the United States of America

DOI: http://dx.doi.org/10.3998/mpub.11356464

ISBN 978-1-60785-507-1 (paper)
ISBN 978-1-60785-508-8 (e-book)
ISBN 978-1-60785-576-7 (OA)

An imprint of Michigan Publishing, Maize Books serves the publishing needs of the University of Michigan community by making high-quality scholarship widely available in print and online. It represents a new model for authors seeking to share their work within and beyond the academy, offering streamlined selection, production, and distribution processes. Maize Books is intended as a complement to more formal modes of publication in a wide range of disciplinary areas.
http://www.maizebooks.org

To my mom and my dad:
two great teachers, two even better parents

A writer, like any athlete, must "train" every day. What did I do today to keep in form?

—Susan Sontag, *As Consciousness Is Harnessed to Flesh: Journals and Notebooks, 1964–1980* (2012)

Writing a paper a week sucks. Getting a B- on my papers sucks. But I am getting better and that feels good. I am excited to see where I am by the end of this.

—University of Michigan student midway through a semester of The Syntax of Sports

Contents

Author's Note

I first taught The Syntax of Sports to several different sections of undergraduates at the University of Michigan, and I continue to use the materials with the law students I work with both at Michigan and at the University of Chicago. The content in this book represents my best effort to re-create the first day of that undergraduate class—or rather what I would want the first day to cover now that I have the benefit of pedagogical hindsight.

To help aid my memory, I have relied on recordings of the class, my own notes, and many helpful conversations with current and former students. I have taken a similar approach when writing each of the subsequent books in this multi-volume *Syntax of Sports* series. Materials related to all of those books—the next of which should be released by 2020—can be found at http://libguides.law.umich.edu/syntax_sports/home.

Acknowledgments

The best part of writing this book has been remembering the classroom conversations that inspired it. They didn't necessarily know it at the time, but each of the students who took "The Syntax of Sports" has turned out to be a wonderful kind of co-author. I am grateful to them all.

I am also grateful to the many people who have helped edit the materials from that course into something that folks who never took it can nevertheless use and enjoy. These include Tyler Berndt, Taylor Brook, Nick Cagle, Christina Cincilla, James Coatsworth, Becca Garfinkle, Michael Goldenberg, Jesse Hogin, Myles Johnson, Akash Patel, Jose Peralta, Darien Perry, Scotti Petterson, Lydia Pincsak, Dimitra Rallis, Matthew Ramirez, Stephen Rees, André Rouillard, Gabrielle Sines, Kimiko Varner, Barb Vibbert, Sage Wen, and Justin Wooten. Every one of them significantly improved this project.

As for the speed and skill with which a collection of notes on my computer transformed into an actual book, the credit for that goes to Jason Colman, Amanda Karby, and the rest of the group at Maize Books, which includes, through a helpful partnership, the editorial production experts at Scribe. A big reason I am excited that *The Syntax of Sports* will be a multi-volume series is that it means I'll get to continue working with all of these people. Publishing is a team sport. I feel very lucky to get to play on theirs.

Class Roster

Below is a class roster, with each student's major listed as a helpful identifying feature. None of the students listed perfectly matches someone who has taken the course. There are too many of them to include. Plus, I wanted to make sure to respect everyone's privacy.

But I will share a nice story about one of the students. His first class in college was the initial session of The Syntax of Sports. (I originally taught it to freshmen.) He then took another course with me, The Syntax of Slavery, and eventually applied to law school. I happily wrote him a recommendation letter.

His first choice was to stay at Michigan, which he ended up doing. So for three more years, I had the pleasure of seeing him grow and develop, from my position as a member of the law school's faculty.

Then, in the final semester of his final year of law school, he signed up for one of my courses, Editing and Advocacy. Because the last class of that course also fell on the last day of the semester, a nice education bookend resulted: his first class at Michigan as an undergraduate and his last class at Michigan as a law student were taught by the same person (me).

The seven years in between are a nice reminder of a writing principle a future volume of *The Syntax of Sports* will cover: end where you began.

Patrick Barry, September 2019

CLASS ROSTER

Teacher
Professor Patrick Barry

Student	*Major*
Ms. Amos	Psychology
Ms. Bart	Business
Mr. Boh	Engineering
Ms. Bristol	Kinesiology
Ms. Burke	Political Science
Mr. Carlos	Biochemistry
Ms. Carroll	Math
Ms. Cawlow	Art History
Mr. Dewey	Education
Mr. Farnoff	American Studies
Ms. Franzoni	History
Ms. Henrietta	Communications
Ms. Ida	Communications
Mr. Leigh	Film
Ms. Maat	Biology
Mr. Marshall	Political Science
Ms. Nina	Music
Ms. Toth	English / Creative Writing
Ms. Yona	Comparative Literature
Ms. Warsaw	Chemistry / Physics
Mr. Wild	English

1

America's Team

Prof. Barry: Ms. Bristol.

Ms. Bristol: Yes.

Prof. Barry: Can you tell us another name for the Dallas Cowboys?

Ms. Bristol: Another name?

Prof. Barry: Yeah. What do people sometimes call the Dallas Cowboys other than just "the Dallas Cowboys"? Here's a hint: the name is kind of patriotic.

Ms. Bristol: Oh. "America's Team." People sometimes call the Dallas Cowboys "America's Team."

Prof. Barry: Good. Now can you tell us another name for the game of baseball? This name is also kind of patriotic.

Ms. Bristol: Yeah. "America's pastime." Baseball is "America's pastime."

Prof. Barry: Good. So here's my real question: Why doesn't "America's Team" play "America's pastime"?

Ms. Bristol: I don't know. I guess . . .

Prof. Barry: Or how about this one: How many teams are in the Big Ten, the conference Michigan plays in? Is it ten or not ten?

Ms. Bristol: Not ten.

Prof. Barry: And how many teams are in the Big 12—the conference Michigan sometimes plays against? Is it twelve or not twelve?

Ms. Bristol: Not twelve.

Prof. Barry: That's kind of weird, right? To name a conference after a certain number of teams and then not have the conference be made up of that number of teams?

Ms. Bristol: Yeah, it's kind of weird.

Prof. Barry: I have a friend who always gives me a hard time about that.

Ms. Bristol: About the Big Ten not having ten teams?

Prof. Barry: Yeah. She went to Michigan, and she loves the school. But she just doesn't get some of the terminology, especially when it comes to sports.

Here's another. You know March Madness?

Ms. Bristol: Yeah.

Prof. Barry: What is the most famous part of March Madness?

Ms. Bristol: The Final Four.

Prof. Barry: And in what month is the Final Four generally played, at least in recent years?

Ms. Bristol: April.

Prof. Barry: Right. April. The most famous part of *March* Madness doesn't actually take place in March. Which is sort of like having Super Bowl Sunday on a Tuesday.

I'm playing around a bit, but the point is that there are some interesting linguistic curiosities to explore once you start looking at the relationship between sports and language.

Ms. Bristol: Is that what we are going to talk about in this course?

Prof. Barry: Sometimes, yeah. But mostly we are going to talk about writing, because as you make your way through college and out into the wider world, you're going to have to write. A lot.

You are going to have to write papers. You are going to have to write memos. You are going to have to write emails, and text messages, and social media posts. In ways large and small, your life will very much be shaped by written words—so I want to make sure you all become good with them.

Skilled writers can connect with people. They can express themselves. They can persuade, encourage, explain, critique, and protest.

Of all the things you can learn from me, the ability to write is perhaps the most important. Do it right, we'll see, and it's like developing a superpower.

2

Good Writing

Prof. Barry: To better understand this superpower, it might be good to get a sense of what good writing both looks like and sounds like—which means we should set out some definitions, however tentative, of what we even mean by "good writing."

Maybe you could help us out with that, Mr. Wild. I think I read in the résumé you submitted that you're an English major. Is that right?

Mr. Wild: Yeah, that's right.

Prof. Barry: Great. So would you mind reading some definitions of good writing as they appear on the PowerPoint slide? That, by the way, is something all of you will be doing a lot this semester.

Mr. Wild: Reading off of PowerPoint slides?

Prof. Barry: Yeah. The class will go a lot better if I'm not the only doing the talking.

Mr. Wild: Got it.

Prof. Barry: Do you see that first definition of good writing at the top of the screen?

Mr. Wild: Yeah.

Prof. Barry: Let's start with that.

Mr. Wild: "Good writing is the best words in their best order."

Prof. Barry: Now the second definition.

Mr. Wild: "Good writing is getting something right in language."

Prof. Barry: And finally, the third.

Mr. Wild: "Good writing is making order out of chaos."

Prof. Barry: Great. We'll come back to each of these definitions in a little bit. But let's first see some good writing in action, starting with a couple of headlines written after the 2013 Outback Bowl between the University of Michigan Wolverines and the University of South Carolina Gamecocks, a college football game that we are going to call "The Ouch-Back Bowl."

3

The Ouch-Back Bowl

Prof. Barry: Where's Mr. Boh?

Mr. Boh: Here.

Prof. Barry: Good. I saw that you listed "tailgating" in the hobbies section of the résumé you submitted. I'm guessing that means you're a big Michigan football fan?

Mr. Boh: I am.

Prof. Barry: You watch all the games?

Mr. Boh: I do.

Prof. Barry: Including the bowl games?

Mr. Boh: Including the bowl games.

Prof. Barry: Did you watch the bowl game Michigan played in 2013 against the South Carolina Gamecocks? The official title was the 2013 Outback Bowl.

Mr. Boh: Unfortunately.

Prof. Barry: I'm guessing from your answer that you can help explain why we, as proud Michigan Wolverines, might instead call the 2013 Outback Bowl the 2013 "Ouch-Back Bowl"?

Mr. Boh: I can try.

Prof. Barry: Great. Take a shot at why the Ouch-Back Bowl may be, for us, a more appropriate name of that game.

Mr. Boh: The game hurt a little.

Prof. Barry: In what way did it hurt a little?

Mr. Boh: It hurt a little in that Michigan played well most of the game.

Prof. Barry: We ran well?

Mr. Boh: Yeah.

Prof. Barry: We passed well?

Mr. Boh: Yeah.

Prof. Barry: And with just five minutes to go in the game, we were actually ahead, weren't we?

Mr. Boh: Yeah.

Prof. Barry: How about with four minutes to go?

Mr. Boh: Still ahead.

Prof. Barry: Three?

Mr. Boh: Still ahead.

Prof. Barry: Two?

Mr. Boh: Still ahead.

Prof. Barry: One?

Mr. Boh: Still ahead.

Prof. Barry: How about with twelve seconds? Were we still ahead then?

Mr. Boh: I think so, yeah.

Prof. Barry: But then?

Mr. Boh: We lost.

Prof. Barry: In the last twelve seconds?

Mr. Boh: Yup.

Prof. Barry: And that hurt a little?

Mr. Boh: I revise my answer. That hurt a lot.

Prof. Barry: Good. Losing like that did hurt a lot, which is one reason why we might refer to that Outback Bowl as the "Ouch-Back Bowl." But there is a second reason as well. Let's bring Ms. Bristol back into the conversation to help us learn about it.

4

Clowney

Prof. Barry: So, Ms. Bristol.

Ms. Bristol: Yeah.

Prof. Barry: Mr. Boh just gave us one explanation for why we might call the 2013 Outback Bowl the "Ouch-Back Bowl."

Ms. Bristol: He did.

Prof. Barry: Can you think of another? Here's a hint: it involves a near decapitation.

Ms. Bristol: You mean the hit by Clowney?

Prof. Barry: I do. You want to tell everyone who you mean by "Clowney"?

Ms. Bristol: Sure. Jadeveon Clowney was South Carolina's beast of a defensive end. Six foot six, two hundred forty pounds, as fast and agile as a wide receiver—and he pretty much knocked the head off of our running back.

Prof. Barry: Do you remember the running back's name?

Ms. Bristol: Wasn't it Vincent Smith?

Prof. Barry: It was. During that game, Clowney—who, by the way, would go on to become the first pick in the 2015 NFL draft and an All-Pro linebacker—did indeed pretty much knock the head off of Vincent Smith. Do you remember the play?

Ms. Bristol: Yeah. At some point in the fourth quarter, Clowney rushed into Michigan's backfield unblocked.

Prof. Barry: Where was Smith?

Ms. Bristol: Getting the handoff.

Prof. Barry: Until?

Ms. Bristol: Clowney tackled him so hard that Smith's helmet actually popped off.

Prof. Barry: Good. So that's the second reason why that game hurt a little, especially if we remember that highlight shows like *SportsCenter* kept playing Clowney's hit over and over and over again.

Ms. Bristol: Right.

Prof. Barry: With that hurt in mind, let's turn to the headline that appeared in the *Detroit Free Press* the day after the game. Read it for us, please, Ms. Henrietta. We'll make use of your journalism skills—you're one of the students who writes for the *Michigan Daily*, right?

Ms. Henrietta: Yeah.

Prof. Barry: There's a second student, too: Ms. Ida. Is she here today?

Ms. Ida: Yeah. I'm here.

Prof. Barry: Great. We'll get you both involved with this headline. Let's start with Ms. Henrietta.

Ms. Henrietta: Okay.

Prof. Barry: Here it is.

Ms. Henrietta: "Gamecocks' Big-Play Capabilities Produce a Bitter Ending for Wolverines' Season."

Prof. Barry: What I want you to help explain, Ms. Henrietta, is why this headline is an example of "good writing," by which I mean the author does an excellent job thinking through two questions:

- Who is the audience of this headline?
- What is the function of this headline?

As the semester moves along, we will give more content to the terms *audience* and *function*. In many ways, they are the two most important terms of the course. In fact, if you take away nothing else from The Syntax of Sports, take away this: whenever you sit down to write anything from a research paper, to a business memo, to a tweet, ask yourself, first, an audience question:

- Who will be reading the words I write?

And then a function question:

- What do I want my words to do?

For now, though, let's just focus on the first question, the question of audience.

Ms. Henrietta: Okay.

Prof. Barry: One way to think about audience is to compare two separate audiences and see how the words you would use to connect with one of them might be different than the words you would use to connect with the other. So let's compare how the audience of the *Detroit Free Press* is different than the audience of the *Charleston Post and Courier*. Both papers covered the 2013 Outback Bowl. But, as we are about to see, they each framed the outcome of the game in very different ways.

5

Audience and Function

Prof. Barry: Compared to the audience of the *Charleston Post and Courier*, Ms. Henrietta, is the audience of the *Detroit Free Press* more or less likely to live in the state of Michigan?

Ms. Henrietta: Compared to the audience of the *Charleston Post and Courier*, the audience of the headline in the *Detroit Free Press* is *more* likely to live in the state of Michigan.

Prof. Barry: And compared to the audience of the *Charleston Post and Courier*, is the audience of the *Detroit Free Press* more or less likely to root for the University of Michigan football team?

Ms. Henrietta: Compared to the audience of the *Charleston Post and Courier*, the audience of the *Detroit Free Press* is *more* likely to root for the University of Michigan football team.

Prof. Barry: So then connect the dots. Why is "Gamecocks' Big-Play Capabilities Produce a Bitter Ending for Wolverines' Season" such a good headline for the audience you described? Why is it "good writing," at least by our current criteria?

Ms. Henrietta: It's good writing because it speaks directly to its audience. It knows that for most readers of the *Detroit Free Press*, watching Michigan lose in the final seconds was pretty painful.

Or as Mr. Boh put it, watching Michigan lose in the final seconds "hurt." A lot.

Prof. Barry: And knowing that, what does the headline do?

Ms. Henrietta: It refers to the end of the game as "bitter."

Prof. Barry: So it captures Mr. Boh's hurt, right?

Ms. Henrietta: Yeah.

Prof. Barry: Which is another way of saying that the headline carries out a specific *function*—our second important term to keep in mind, along with *audience*. Rarely in this course will I ask you to tell me what anything you write is *about*. I'm not really interested in what your writing is *about*. What I am interested in is what your paper is *trying to do*. What I am interested in is the kind of "action in words" your writing is, to use a phrase often said by one of my own teachers.

What I am interested in, fundamentally, is *function*. Because as we will see in a moment, two pieces of writing can be "about" the same thing—in our case, the same football game—but have two completely different functions. And if you don't know that as a writer, then you are going to have a hard time being effective.

6

Thrilling

Prof. Barry: It's time to bring you into the conversation, Ms. Ida.

Ms. Ida: Okay.

Prof. Barry: We just learned from Ms. Henrietta that the headline "Gamecocks' Big-Play Capabilities Produce a Bitter Ending for Wolverines' Season" is an example of good writing.

Ms. Ida: Right.

Prof. Barry: And when Ms. Henrietta explained why that headline is an example of good writing, she focused on the word *bitter*. She said the word performed an important function: it captured the hurt felt by Michigan fans as they watched their team snatch defeat from the jaws of victory.

Ms. Ida: Yeah.

Prof. Barry: Can you say a little bit more about what she might have meant? Why is the word *bitter* so essential to the success of the headline?

Ms. Ida: I think without "bitter," you might lose the hurt.

Prof. Barry: So if you replace "bitter" with another word . . .

Ms. Ida: Yeah, if you replace it with a word that's more neutral.

Prof. Barry: For example?

Ms. Ida: I don't know. Something less obviously negative.

Prof. Barry: Like?

Ms. Ida: Maybe "dramatic"?

Prof. Barry: "Dramatic"?

Ms. Ida: Yeah. "Dramatic."

Prof. Barry: So the headline would read "Gamecocks' Big-Play Capabilities Produce a Dramatic Ending for Wolverines' Season." And you think that with that change, with that edit, we lose the hurt?

Ms. Ida: I think so. I think "Gamecocks' Big-Play Capabilities Produce a Dramatic Ending for Wolverines' Season" is a lot different than "Gamecocks' Big-Play Capabilities Produce a Bitter Ending for Wolverines' Season." The word *dramatic* doesn't communicate the same feeling of disappointment.

Prof. Barry: Because there are things that are "dramatic" that are good . . .

Ms. Ida: Yeah. And there are things that are "dramatic" that are bad.

Prof. Barry: The word is too ambiguous.

Ms. Ida: Right. The word is too ambiguous.

Prof. Barry: How about "Gamecocks' Big-Play Capabilities Produce a Wild Ending for Wolverines' Season"?

Ms. Ida: Same problem.

Prof. Barry: "Gamecocks Big-Play Capabilities Produce an Unexpected Ending for Wolverines' Season"?

Ms. Ida: Nope.

Prof. Barry: Or how about this? "Gamecocks' Big-Play Capabilities Produce a Thrilling Ending for Wolverines' Season?"

Ms. Ida: That'd be terrible.

Prof. Barry: Why?

Ms. Ida: Because you'd be telling a bunch of Michigan fans, "Look, you just had your heart broken. How *thrilling*!"

Prof. Barry: That's a tough sell?

Ms. Ida: Very.

Prof. Barry: But what if the audience were South Carolina fans?

Ms. Ida: That'd be different. For South Carolina fans, it might actually be "thrilling" to have a game break the hearts of Michigan fans.

Prof. Barry: You think?

Ms. Ida: Yeah. I kind of do.

Prof. Barry: Well, the editors of the *Charleston Post and Courier*—the newspaper we mentioned that caters to South Carolina fans—appear to have thought so too. They actually included the word *thrilling* when describing that year's Outback Bowl. Do you mind reading the full headline for us, Ms. Ida? It appeared on the same day that the headline "Gamecocks' Big-Play Capabilities Produce a Bitter Ending for Wolverines' Season" appeared in the *Detroit Free Press*.

Ms. Ida: "South Carolina Beats Michigan 33–28 in Thrilling Outback Bowl."

Prof. Barry: Notice the difference. In the *Detroit Free Press*, a paper that targets Michigan fans, the headline was "Gamecocks' Big-Play Capabilities Produce Bitter Ending to Wolverines' Season." And in the *Charleston Post and Courier*, a paper that targets South Carolina fans, the headline was, "South Carolina Beats Michigan 33–28 in Thrilling Outback Bowl."

Yet—and this is really important—these two very different-sounding headlines describe the exact same game. There are no factual discrepancies between the headlines. Nor are there any in the accompanying articles. In terms of raw data, the two give identical information: South Carolina scored thirty-three points in the 2013 Outback Bowl, and Michigan scored twenty-eight.

The framing, however, the language used to take control of and characterize the game—now that, Ms. Ida, is what's different. Very, very different. Because?

Ms. Ida: The audience is different.

Prof. Barry: And?

Ms. Ida: The function is different.

Prof. Barry: Exactly. One way to think about the headline in the *Detroit Free Press* is that its function is to define that particular Outback Bowl—for an audience full of Wolverine fans—as a Michigan defeat. "Look," it's saying, "Michigan lost that game."

Ms. Ida: Right.

Prof. Barry: Just as one way to think about the headline in the *Charleston Post and Courier* is that its function is to define that same game—for an audience full of Gamecocks fans—as a South Carolina victory. "Michigan didn't lose that game," we might say, based on the *Post and Courier* headline. "No, no. South Carolina *won*!"

Ms. Ida: The difference being?

Prof. Barry: Let's turn to Daniel Kahneman to help us answer that.

7

Writing, Fast and Slow

Prof. Barry: Ms. Amos.

Ms. Amos: Yes.

Prof. Barry: Your résumé says you're majoring in psychology.

Ms. Amos: Yup.

Prof. Barry: So have you ever heard of Daniel Kahneman?

Ms. Amos: I have.

Prof. Barry: Who is he?

Ms. Amos: A Nobel Prize winner.

Prof. Barry: In?

Ms. Amos: Economics.

Prof. Barry: Even though?

Ms. Amos: He's not an economist.

Prof. Barry: Right. He was actually trained as a psychologist. So all through college and graduate school, he studied what you're studying.

Ms. Amos: Right.

Prof. Barry: Yet he eventually won a Nobel Prize in an entirely different field.

Ms. Amos: Yeah.

Prof. Barry: Which is sort of like a golfer winning Wimbledon.

Ms. Amos: I guess.

Prof. Barry: Or a soccer player winning the Tour de France.

Ms. Amos: I don't know if I would go that far.

Prof. Barry: Fine. But it is still pretty impressive.

Ms. Amos: Definitely.

Prof. Barry: Another thing that's impressive: Kahneman's best-selling book *Thinking, Fast and Slow*. It was picked as a Best Book of the Year by the *Economist*, by the *Wall Street Journal*, by the *New York Times Book Review*—by a whole bunch of publications.

We'll soon look at an excerpt from it that will help us better understand the framing move involved in saying "Michigan lost" versus "South Carolina won." But first I want to talk about a different example.

Ms. Amos: Okay.

Prof. Barry: Do you know what the Ryder Cup is?

Ms. Amos: Isn't it some sort of golf event?

Prof. Barry: Yup. Between players from the US and players from Europe. It's one of the few times when golf turns into a team sport.

Ms. Amos: And it doesn't happen every year, right?

Prof. Barry: Right. It happens every two years. The one I want to talk about took place back in 2012, at a wonderful golf course in Medinah,

Illinois. The US team got off to a really great start and entered the final day with the seemingly insurmountable lead of 10–6.

Ms. Amos: Is the Ryder Cup always in the US?

Prof. Barry: No. The teams alternate hosting so that neither keeps having a home-course advantage.

Ms. Amos: Is that really a thing in golf?

Prof. Barry: Home-course advantage?

Ms. Amos: Yeah.

Prof. Barry: It seemed to be in 2012. The US team took a commanding lead during the first three days of the four-day competition. To overcome it, the Europeans had to eliminate a final-day deficit as large as any in the Ryder Cup's then eighty-five-year history.

Ms. Bristol (*jumping in*): I remember watching that Ryder Cup with my dad. It was heartbreaking.

Prof. Barry: Because?

Ms. Bristol: The US team had a complete meltdown on that fourth and final day. They couldn't make a putt. They couldn't find a fairway. They couldn't do anything.

Prof. Barry: They choked.

Ms. Bristol: Yeah. They choked. On one of the biggest stages in golf. It was terrible.

Prof. Barry: So I actually have, on the next slide, a headline from the *Washington Post* soon after the "meltdown" you mentioned. Would you mind reading it for us, Ms. Bristol? It captures the experience you and your dad had as viewers. It even uses your word.

Ms. Bristol: *Meltdown*?

Prof. Barry: Yeah. Here it is.

Ms. Bristol: "Ryder Cup: Who's to Blame for the Medinah Meltdown?"

Prof. Barry: But now let's think about what that same Ryder Cup looked like from the perspective of the Europeans. To them, the final day wasn't a "meltdown," was it?

Ms. Bristol: No. It was a miracle.

Prof. Barry: "The Miracle at Medinah."

Ms. Bristol: Yeah. The Miracle at Medinah. That's how the Europeans are going to remember it.

Prof. Barry: Not as an American collapse?

Ms. Bristol: No. As a European comeback.

Prof. Barry: Maybe even as a comeback of "epic proportions"?

Ms. Bristol: Maybe.

Prof. Barry: I say that because I now want you to read the Ryder Cup headline used in the *Guardian*, a London-based newspaper whose audience includes a lot of Europeans.

Ms. Bristol: "Europe Seal Ryder Cup Win with Comeback of Epic Proportions."

Prof. Barry: Kind of a different take than the *Washington Post*, right?

Ms. Bristol: Yeah. It's the opposite take.

Prof. Barry: That's right. It's the opposite take. So now here's a question: Which headline is more true?

Ms. Bristol: Between the *Washington Post* and the headline in the *Guardian*?

Prof. Barry: Yeah. Was the 2012 Ryder Cup a comeback of epic proportions, or was it a collapse of epic proportions? Are the events that day better described as "The Miracle at Medinah" or as "The Meltdown at Medinah"? Or let's return to the language we used when talking about the 2013 Outback Bowl between Michigan and South Carolina. When all is said and done, did the Europeans win the 2012 Ryder Cup or did the Americans lose it?

Ms. Bristol: I think both, kind of.

Prof. Barry: Smart answer. There is definitely a way in which each statement is equally true, depending on the audience. For some folks, the Europeans won. For others, the Americans lost.

Either way, I hope we are starting to understand the power language gives us to reframe reality. With it, you can take a glorious comeback and say, "Wait, hold on a second, this was actually—or at least also—an inglorious collapse." And just as significantly, you can take a miracle and say, "Slow down. Perhaps it's better to think of this as a meltdown."

Ms. Bristol: Right.

Prof. Barry: This power is perhaps the most important thing about writing and language that I can teach you. It has big-time implications for those of you who may someday frame a legal case or pitch a product. It has big-time implications for those of you who may someday deliver bad news to a child or try to motivate a friend. And it certainly has big-time implications for anyone who, as a doctor, may someday talk about medical risks with a patient. Is it better to say, for example, "Sir, you have a 90 percent chance of making it through this surgery" or "Sir, you have a 10 percent chance of not making it through this surgery"? Is it better to focus on survival rates or mortality rates?

Or take a more ordinary situation. Suppose you are trying to get people to register for an event. Say it's a conference, a race, a charity ball, whatever, and you want everyone to sign up before a particular date. Should you tell them that the registration fee will be cheaper if they sign up before the date or that it will be more expensive if they sign up after the date? Should you talk in terms of discounts or surcharges? Bonuses or penalties?

Ms. Bristol: That's a framing decision?

Prof. Barry: Yeah. That's a framing decision. And so is, a bit more playfully, the reorientation implicit in Winston Churchill's famous remark that a pessimist is someone who finds difficulty in every opportunity, while an optimist is someone who finds opportunity in every difficulty. Or in the writer G. K. Chesterton's observation that an inconvenience is an adventure wrongly considered while an adventure is an inconvenience rightly considered.

Ms. Bristol: I like that last one.

Prof. Barry: From G. K. Chesterton?

Ms. Bristol: Yeah, I think I'll use it the next time I get lost. "I'm not lost," I'll tell myself. "I'm not even inconvenienced. I am simply on *an adventure*!"

Prof. Barry: I'm not sure that will go over well if you're with another person. But here's something I *am* sure of: it is really important that we all learn just how flexible—and consequential—language can be.

Which brings us back to Daniel Kahneman. We haven't forgotten about him.

8

Italy Won, France Lost

Prof. Barry: What Kahneman does, Ms. Amos, is helpfully explain the mechanics of framing. The passage I'd like you to read comes from the book *Thinking, Fast and Slow* I mentioned earlier. Would you mind reading it for us? The subject is the 2006 World Cup soccer final between Italy and France.

Ms. Amos: "Italy and France competed in the 2006 World Cup. The next two sentences both describe the outcome: Italy won. France lost."

Prof. Barry: Good. Here's the question Kahneman asks: Do those statements—"Italy won" and "France Lost"—mean the same thing?

On the level of pure data, Kahneman points out—a level stripped of emotion and story and connotation—of course the statements mean the same thing. One team losing a game is the same thing as the other team winning. But on a more human level—a level of images and nuance and imagination, of words being able to change the world people see—the statements actually mean very different things. Let's keep reading, Ms. Amos.

Ms. Amos: "Italy won evokes thoughts of the Italian team and what it did to win."

Prof. Barry: So you read or hear "Italy won" and you think of what, Ms. Bristol? I'm switching back to you because your résumé says you actually play on the soccer team here at Michigan.

Ms. Bristol: I do.

Prof. Barry: Does that mean you also watch soccer? Do you watch the World Cup, for example, when it comes on every four years?

Ms. Bristol: Yup.

Prof. Barry: Did you watch it in 2006?

Ms. Bristol: I did.

Prof. Barry: Including the final between Italy and France?

Ms. Bristol: Yeah. That's the first World Cup I remember watching. My whole family got into it.

Prof. Barry: Great. That will make my job a lot easier, because what I want you to do now is think back to that match.

Ms. Bristol: Okay.

Prof. Barry: What might the phrase "Italy won" make your mind focus on as you mentally recap the game?

Ms. Bristol: I guess Italy coming back to tie the game at 1-1 after giving up an early goal.

Prof. Barry: What else?

Ms. Bristol: Maybe their goalkeeper.

Prof. Barry: Gianluigi Buffon?

Ms. Bristol: Yeah, him—Buffon. I remember Buffon making that key save in extra time to send the match into penalty kicks. Wasn't that him?

Prof. Barry: Yeah. He saved a really powerful header by France from close range.

Ms. Bristol: Oh, and also how all five of the Italians who took a penalty kick made their penalty kicks. I might focus on that.

Prof. Barry: So essentially, you'd focus on the story of the match from—?

Ms. Bristol: Italy's point of view.

Prof. Barry: What about with "<u>France lost</u>"?

Ms. Bristol: Probably the opposite. I'd probably focus on the match from France's point of view.

Prof. Barry: For example?

Ms. Bristol: I'd think of some of their mistakes.

Prof. Barry: The penalty shot of David Trezeguet, France's star forward, hitting the crossbar?

Ms. Bristol: Probably.

Prof. Barry: The head-butt by Zinedine Zidane?

Ms. Bristol: Definitely.

Prof. Barry: Why definitely?

Ms. Bristol: Because it earned him a red card.

Prof. Barry: Which meant?

Ms. Bristol: He got ejected and France had to play the last minutes of the match with only ten players.

Prof. Barry: What else did it mean—particularly for the penalty shootout at the end?

Ms. Bristol: That France was without its best penalty taker. It was a really devastating red card.

Prof. Barry: Kahneman agrees with you, particularly about Zidane. Please read the next little bit from his book.

Ms. Amos: "France lost evokes thoughts of the French team and what it did to lose, including the memorable head-butt of an Italian player by the French star Zinedine Zidane."

Prof. Barry: And now, summing up Kahneman's comparison of the two sentences—"Italy won" versus "France lost."

Ms. Amos: "In terms of the association they bring to mind, the two sentences really 'mean' different things."

Prof. Barry: Isn't that pretty cool? Kahneman teaches us that just by choosing a different set of words and changing the frame, we can alter how people process an event—and so by extension, how they process the world. That's the power of language.

9

Losing Gold

Prof. Barry: Nike provides another good example of this power. And so does, interestingly enough, Amy Poehler.

Ms. Amos: The comedian?

Prof. Barry: Yeah. But let's begin with Nike. You want to get us started, Ms. Bart? Your résumé says you're a BBA student over at the Ross School of Business. So is it safe to assume that you know at least a little bit about marketing?

Ms. Bart: Yeah, I know a little bit. I took a marketing course last term.

Prof. Barry: Good. Let's now add to that knowledge by talking about a clever ad campaign Nike put together back in 1996 for that year's Summer Olympics in Atlanta.

Ms. Bart: Okay.

Prof. Barry: The function of the campaign was to stress that the athletes Nike sponsored weren't at the Olympics just to compete and share in the spirit of athletic grace, excellence, and camaraderie. They were there to win. More specifically, they were there for gold.

So Nike put together a commercial centered on Lisa Leslie, a star of the women's basketball team. It was about thirty seconds long.

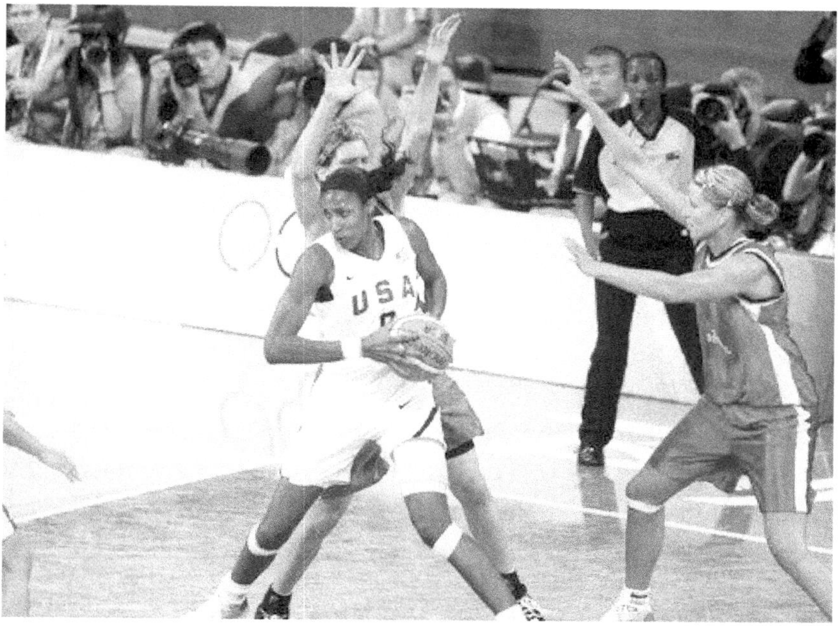

And after, say, twenty-five seconds of Leslie rebounding, dunking, and generally performing like the Olympic champion she would soon become, a voice comes on and says the following.

Ms. Bart: "You don't win silver. You lose gold."

Prof. Barry: So tell us, Ms. Bart, what sort of framing move was Nike pulling there?

Ms. Bart: The kind that says winning a silver medal is no victory at all. It's actually a defeat.

Prof. Barry: And why is it a defeat?

Ms. Bart: The person could have, maybe even should have, won gold.

Prof. Barry: Exactly. Nike takes this amazing achievement—winning a silver medal—and reframes it as a letdown, as not good enough, as, essentially, failure.

Ms. Bart: Right.

Prof. Barry: Of course, that's not the only way to frame that kind of result. Suppose you had a situation in which a team that people thought was good but not unbeatable played great in the early rounds of a tournament and also played great in the later rounds, including the Round of 16, and the quarterfinals, and the semifinals—but then, when they got to the finals, they met a team that played just a little bit better.

Ms. Bart: Okay.

Prof. Barry: What might you change about the language of the Nike ad so that you could now focus on how, in these new circumstances, coming in second place is really a cause for celebration, that it's something about which the team—and its fans—should be proud?

Ms. Bart: I'd start by scrapping the "lose gold" line.

Prof. Barry: What would you replace it with?

Ms. Bart: Well, maybe I'd actually keep it.

Prof. Barry: Yeah?

Ms. Bart: Yeah, I'd keep it.

Prof. Barry: So then what would you change?

Ms. Bart: Maybe I'd just change the order. Instead of saying "You don't win silver. You lose gold," I'd say . . .

Prof. Barry: "You don't lose gold. You win silver"?

Ms. Bart: Yeah.

Prof. Barry: Great. That's what I was hoping you'd come up with because the *Detroit Free Press* once wrote something very similar in a headline right at the end of March Madness, as we are about to see.

10

Winning Silver

Prof. Barry: Mr. Boh.

Mr. Boh: Yes.

Prof. Barry: Earlier we learned that you're a fan of Michigan football. Are you also a fan of Michigan basketball?

Mr. Boh: I'm a fan of Michigan everything.

Prof. Barry: So I take it you watched March Madness in 2013?

Mr. Boh: I did.

Prof. Barry: How much of it?

Mr. Boh: Pretty much all of it.

Prof. Barry: Why?

Mr. Boh: Because Michigan kept winning.

Prof. Barry: Were we expected to?

Mr. Boh: Not really.

Prof. Barry: How come?

Mr. Boh: We were only a number four seed in our bracket, and ten other teams were ranked higher than us overall. We were also, I think, the youngest team in the tournament.

Prof. Barry: But?

Mr. Boh: We played great in the early rounds.

Prof. Barry: And?

Mr. Boh: We played great in the later rounds.

Prof. Barry: Including the Sweet Sixteen?

Mr. Boh: Yup.

Prof. Barry: And the Elite Eight?

Mr. Boh: Yup.

Prof. Barry: And the Final Four?

Mr. Boh: Yup.

Prof. Barry: So Michigan made it all the way to the championship game.

Mr. Boh: Right.

Prof. Barry: Who did we face there?

Mr. Boh: Louisville.

Prof. Barry: Which was?

Mr. Boh: The best team in the country.

Prof. Barry: By which you mean?

Mr. Boh: They were ranked number one in their bracket, and they were also ranked number one overall.

Prof. Barry: Did Louisville play a little bit better than Michigan in that championship game?

Mr. Boh: Unfortunately.

Prof. Barry: So Michigan lost. They didn't get first place.

Mr. Boh: Right. They got second place.

Prof. Barry: So if the *Detroit Free Press* had followed the lead of Nike when crafting its headline for the morning after that final game, it could have written this.

Mr. Boh: "You don't win second place. You lose first place."

Prof. Barry: Do you think the *Detroit Free Press* wrote that, Mr. Boh?

Mr. Boh: Probably not.

Prof. Barry: Why?

Mr. Boh: Because that would be mean.

Prof. Barry: Do you want to see the headline the *Detroit Free Press* actually wrote? It's not mean at all.

Mr. Boh: Sure.

Prof. Barry: Here it is. Please read it for the class.

Mr. Boh: "Hail, Hail to the NCAA Runner-Up."

Prof. Barry: Isn't that awesome?

Mr. Boh: Yeah.

Prof. Barry: Explain why. Explain what is so awesome about "Hail, Hail to the NCAA Runner-Up." And start with what is generous about it, since part of why the headline is awesome is that it's generous.

Mr. Boh: It's generous in the sense that the headline takes the focus off the individual loss and reminds everyone—the players, the coaches, the fans—that getting all the way to the NCAA championship game is still a very impressive achievement.

Prof. Barry: Good. Now explain what's clever about "Hail, Hail to the NCAA Runner-Up," since another reason the headline is awesome is that it's also very clever.

Mr. Boh: You mean the "Hail, Hail" part?

Prof. Barry: Yeah.

Mr. Boh: "Hail, Hail" references Michigan's fight song and school motto.

Prof. Barry: "Hail to the Victors," right?

Mr. Boh: Right.

Prof. Barry: So it's an . . .

Mr. Boh: Illusion?

Prof. Barry: Close. A-llusion. "Hail, Hail, to NCAA Runner-Up" is an a-llusion, with an *a*. It *alludes* to the Michigan fight song and motto. Just like the title of William Faulkner's novel *The Sound and the Fury* is an allusion to a famous line in *Macbeth* by William

Shakespeare: "[Life is] a tale told by an idiot, full of sound and fury, signifying nothing."

Mr. Boh: Right. Allusion. I often say that wrong.

Prof. Barry: Later in the term, we'll talk about a different and perhaps more helpful word for an allusion, or at least a certain kind of one: "a culture kick." But for now, let's leave the world of sports so that we can see how language doesn't just help us reframe particular events, like a bowl game or performance in the NCAA tournament; it can also help us reframe particular people, including quite powerful people. The comedian Amy Poehler is going to show us how.

11

Hillary Clinton's Husband

Prof. Barry: Where's Mr. Farnoff?

Mr. Farnoff: Right here.

Prof. Barry: Great. I'm hoping you can tell us a little about Amy Poehler. Your résumé says you're majoring in American culture, and it lists "memoirs by comedians" as one of your interests.

Mr. Farnoff: Yeah. I love those kinds of books.

Prof. Barry: Which ones have you read—*Bossypants* by Tina Fey?

Mr. Farnoff: Yup.

Prof. Barry: *Born Standing Up* by Steve Martin?

Mr. Farnoff: Yup.

Prof. Barry: *Born a Crime* by Trevor Noah?

Mr. Farnoff: Yup.

Prof. Barry: Any others?

Mr. Farnoff: Yeah, a bunch. Mindy Kaling's, Jim Gaffigan's, Jerry Seinfeld's, Billy Crystal's . . .

Prof. Barry: Have you read Amy Poehler's?

Mr. Farnoff: *Yes Please*?

Prof. Barry: Right. *Yes Please*.

Mr. Farnoff: Yeah. I've read it. I was a big fan of her on *Saturday Night Live* and *Parks and Rec*.

Prof. Barry: She has also cohosted the Golden Globes a couple of times.

Mr. Farnoff: Right. With Tina Fey.

Prof. Barry: You remember how they did?

Mr. Farnoff: I think they did pretty well. I still remember one of the jokes Tina Fey told.

Prof. Barry: Yeah?

Mr. Farnoff: Yeah. "*The Hunger Games* is one of the biggest films of the year," she said, "and also what I call the six weeks it took me to get into this dress."

Prof. Barry: Do you remember when former president Bill Clinton appeared on stage to introduce one of the nominees for Best Picture? I think it was *Lincoln*.

Mr. Farnoff: Yeah. I remember that.

Prof. Barry: Remember how he got a huge, positive reaction? People cheered. People applauded. I think the crowd gave him a standing ovation.

Mr. Farnoff: Right.

Prof. Barry: And then Amy Poehler comes out, with the audience still buzzing, and she says the following sentence.

Mr. Farnoff: "Wow, what an exciting special guest. That was ________."

Prof. Barry: Finish it off for us, please.

Mr. Farnoff: "Hillary Clinton's husband."

Prof. Barry: Isn't that brilliant? Amy Poehler could have described Bill Clinton as "the former president of the United States." She could have described him as "a past leader of the free world." She could have described him using any number of terms that would have put Bill and his many accomplishments front and center.

But instead, she essentially said, "Look, the most interesting thing about this guy: he's married to someone even more interesting."

Mr. Farnoff: And this was before the 2016 election, right?

Prof. Barry: Right. About three years before. Still secretary of state at the time, Hillary hadn't even announced her candidacy yet. Or at least not officially.

Mr. Farnoff: That makes the joke even better.

Prof. Barry: I know. But here's the key point: the linguistic choice Poehler made is one we all face anytime we describe someone, including ourselves. Is that *your* boss, or are you *her* employee? Is that *your* girlfriend, or are you *her* boyfriend?

Mr. Wild (*jumping in*): Or maybe we are our boyfriend's boyfriend.

Prof. Barry: Good. Exactly. In each of these examples, and certainly in the one we'll talk about next class involving the baseball great Josh Gibson, how you frame people in relation to other people, how you use language to privilege some folks over other folks—all of this communicates powerful, value-laden packets of information to your audience and may alter how they perceive a given situation. "The words you choose," you'll hear me say over and over again, "can change the world people see."

Which bring us to one of my favorite uses of language ever. It comes from a football game played between two schools not normally known for playing football games: Harvard and Yale.

12

Harvard vs. Yale

Prof. Barry: I have some questions for you, Mr. Dewey—you're in the School of Education, right?

Mr. Dewey: Right.

Prof. Barry: Good. Because my questions are about the two universities I just mentioned: Harvard and Yale.

Mr. Dewey: Okay.

Prof. Barry: Are those two schools known for having powerhouse football programs?

Mr. Dewey: Not exactly.

Prof. Barry: Their teams don't generally appear on *SportsCenter*?

Mr. Dewey: No.

Prof. Barry: They don't make the cover of *Sports Illustrated*?

Mr. Dewey: Not that I've seen.

Prof. Barry: So then it might be a little surprising to hear that when Harvard and Yale played each other back in 1968, Harvard was undefeated with a record of 8–0, and so was Yale.

Mr. Dewey: A little bit, yeah.

Prof. Barry: But let me clarify something: although both Harvard and Yale were undefeated at the time, Yale was the heavy, heavy favorite in that game. And soon into the second quarter, they had already gone up 22–0.

Mr. Leigh (*interrupting*): Wait, I might know about this game. Is there a documentary about it?

Prof. Barry: Yeah. A great documentary.

Mr. Leigh: I think I've seen it. Wasn't Yale's quarterback a big reason Yale was so good? I forgot his name.

Prof. Barry: Dowling. His name is Brian Dowling.

Mr. Leigh: Right. Brian Dowling. I remember the documentary saying that he hadn't lost a game since, like, kindergarten.

Prof. Barry: Close. Seventh grade. Brian Dowling hadn't lost a game since the seventh grade. He wasn't that big. He wasn't that fast. He just apparently knew how to win—and win and win and win. Do you remember, Mr. Leigh, the famous comic strip Dowling ended up appearing in? I think the documentary mentioned it.

Mr. Leigh: Was it *The Far Side*?

Prof. Barry: Nope.

Mr. Leigh: *Peanuts*?

Prof. Barry: Nope.

Mr. Leigh: *Calvin and Hobbes*?

Prof. Barry: Not that either. It was *Doonesbury*. The strip's creator, Gary Trudeau, was a student at Yale when Brian Dowling was the big jock on campus. So one of the *Doonesbury* characters is a guy named "B. D."

Mr. Leigh: For Brian Dowling?

Prof. Barry: Yeah. He wears a football uniform stamped with the number 10, which was Dowling's number. He also wears a helmet with the Yale logo. And in one strip, a woman drawn to be a bit of a ditz comes over to him, sees that he's wearing his full uniform and helmet, and says, without any hint of irony, "You play football, am I right?"

Mr. Leigh: That's pretty funny.

Prof. Barry: Isn't it? Trudeau's really clever. But let's go back to this game between Harvard and Yale. Where did we leave off?

Mr. Leigh: You were saying that Yale jumped out to a 22–0 lead.

Prof. Barry: Right. And that was in part because of Brian Dowling. But Yale also had another star player. Do you remember him from the documentary? He tied Yale's record for career touchdowns when he scored one in that game.

Mr. Leigh: Yeah. Calvin Hill.

Prof. Barry: Right. Calvin Hill. And what's notable about Calvin Hill, particularly in terms of where he went after graduating from Yale?

Mr. Leigh: After Yale, he went to the NFL.

Prof. Barry: To run its marketing team?

Mr. Leigh: Nope.

Prof. Barry: To head its legal department?

Mr. Leigh: Nope.

Prof. Barry: To do what, then?

Mr. Leigh: To play wide receiver.

Prof. Barry: That's right. For the Dallas Cowboys. Which we learned at the beginning of class is what?

Mr. Leigh: "America's Team."

13
The Hills

Prof. Barry: Do you think, Mr. Leigh, that a lot of people who graduate from Yale end up playing for the Cowboys or any other NFL team?

Mr. Leigh: Probably not.

Prof. Barry: So that makes Calvin Hill kind of exceptional.

Mr. Leigh: Yeah.

Prof. Barry: Anybody know what else makes him exceptional? It involves his family.

Maybe you, Ms. Bristol? Your résumé screams "sports junkie," and you've done a great job answering questions so far.

Ms. Bristol: Isn't he the father of Grant Hill?

Prof. Barry: Good. And what's notable about Grant Hill?

Ms. Bristol: Grant Hill was a star basketball player.

Prof. Barry: When?

Ms. Bristol: In college, at Duke.

Prof. Barry: And also?

Ms. Bristol: In the NBA, with the Pistons, here in Michigan.

Prof. Barry: Which means an NFL dad who went to Yale—Calvin Hill—produced an NBA son who went to Duke, Grant Hill.

Ms. Bristol: Yeah.

Prof. Barry: Not really a family of underachievers, huh?

Ms. Bristol: No. Not at all.

Prof. Barry: Especially if you factor in that Calvin Hill's wife—and so Grant Hill's mom—went to Wellesley, another elite school. She was friends with Hillary Clinton.

Ms. Bristol: Really?

Prof. Barry: Yeah. And the Clinton connection is only the start of the political pedigree of this amazing Harvard-Yale football game from 1968. But first, we are going to look at the game's Hollywood pedigree, beginning with a certain future Oscar winner at Vassar. Her boyfriend played fullback for Yale.

14

Hollywood

Prof. Barry: Do you remember the fullback I'm talking about, Mr. Leigh? He was in the documentary. His is name is Bob Levin.

Mr. Leigh: Yeah. I remember that guy.

Prof. Barry: Do you also remember how, at one point, Bob Levin talks about the person he was dating back in 1968, the year of the game?

Mr. Leigh: Yup.

Prof. Barry: Who was it?

Mr. Leigh: Meryl Streep.

Mr. Farnoff (*jumping in*)**:** Really? Meryl Streep?

Mr. Leigh: Yeah. Meryl Streep. She was at the Yale School of Drama.

Prof. Barry: Not yet she wasn't. At the time of the game, she was still an undergrad.

Mr. Leigh: At Yale?

Prof. Barry: No, at Vassar. It was an intercollegiate romance. But that's not the only Hollywood connection in the game. There's another one, this time on the Harvard side. Do you remember it, Mr. Leigh?

Mr. Leigh: I think so. It involves one of the Harvard players, right?

Prof. Barry: Yeah. An offensive lineman who went on to become a famous actor.

Mr. Leigh: Right.

Prof. Barry: You want to tell everybody who it was?

Mr. Leigh: Tommy Lee Jones.

Prof. Barry: Exactly. Tommy Lee Jones was an offensive lineman for Harvard and played in the game we've been talking about. Which gives you some idea of the difference between college football in 1968 and college football today.

For example, it is not uncommon for an offensive lineman today to be what, 6′5″, 6′6″?

Mr. Leigh: About that.

Prof. Barry: Remember Michael Oher, the offensive lineman in the movie *The Blindside*?

Mr. Leigh: Yeah. He was a giant.

Prof. Barry: Or think of NFL Hall of Famer Jonathan Ogden. He was 6′9″ and weighed more than three hundred pounds.

Mr. Leigh: Right.

Prof. Barry: Do you think Tommy Lee Jones was 6′9″ in college?

Mr. Leigh: No.

Prof. Barry: Do you think he weighed more than three hundred pounds?

Mr. Leigh: I'd be surprised if he weighed more than two hundred pounds.

Prof. Barry: Me too—though I suppose there is someone we could ask.

Mr. Leigh: Who?

Prof. Barry: His college roommate. He's just as famous as Tommy Lee Jones, maybe even more so. Any idea who he is?

Mr. Leigh: No. I don't think so.

Prof. Barry: Would it help if I told you he won an Oscar?

Mr. Leigh: Is it Matt Damon?

Prof. Barry: Matt Damon did go to Harvard.

Mr. Leigh: And he won an Oscar.

Prof. Barry: Right, for *Good Will Hunting*. But it's not Matt Damon. He's several years younger than Tommy Lee Jones. Plus, he hasn't yet earned a second award the roommate won.

Mr. Leigh: What?

Prof. Barry: A Grammy.

Mr. Leigh: The roommate won an Oscar *and* a Grammy?

Prof. Barry: And the Nobel Peace Prize.

Mr. Leigh: Really? Who is this guy?

Prof. Barry: Well, he was almost elected president once. Does that help?

Mr. Leigh: No. Not at all. I seriously have no idea who this person could be.

Prof. Barry: I think we have a political science major in the class. Perhaps she can help us out. It's Ms. Burke, right?

Ms. Burke: Yeah.

Prof. Barry: So do you know who we're talking about?

Ms. Burke: I think so. I remember hearing that Tommy Lee Jones's roommate ran for president.

Prof. Barry: Do you remember what year?

Ms. Burke: 2000?

Prof. Barry: That's right. So who is it? Who is this very accomplished mystery man?

Ms. Burke: Al Gore?

Prof. Barry: Yup. In addition to winning an Oscar, a Grammy, and the Nobel Peace Prize, Al Gore was also, way back in college, Tommy Lee Jones's roommate.

15

White House

Prof. Barry: Al Gore, however, was not the only other future politician mentioned in the documentary. Do you remember the other one, Mr. Leigh? He was also the roommate of one of the players—but on the Yale side. The roommate's name was Ted Livingston.

Mr. Leigh: I remember Ted Livingston. He played defensive tackle.

Prof. Barry: Right. And how about his roommate?

Mr. Leigh: I remember him too.

Prof. Barry: Good. Who was he?

Mr. Leigh: George W. Bush.

Ms. Burke (*jumping in*)**:** Come on. That can't be right.

Mr. Leigh: Seriously. He was. George W. Bush was the roommate of Ted Livingston.

Prof. Barry: Mr. Leigh is right. After finishing high school at Phillips Academy in Andover, and before getting his MBA from Harvard, Bush was an undergraduate at Yale, right at the time of this football game.

Which means, Mr. Leigh, that there is another way to think about this football game, given that it was played between two ostensibly well-matched opponents, each with a highly loyal, deeply partisan, and probably quite wealthy fan base—including, for Yale, George W. Bush presumably cheering on his roommate Ted Livingston, and for Harvard, Al Gore, presumably cheering on his roommate Tommy Lee Jones.

Mr. Leigh: Right.

Prof. Barry: The game wasn't just "Harvard vs. Yale" or "Yale vs. Harvard." Another way to think about it is?

Mr. Leigh: *Bush v. Gore*.

Prof. Barry: Especially because?

Mr. Leigh: It ended in a tie.

16

Chaos

Prof. Barry: As we said before, Yale jumped to an early 22–0 lead in this game and looked like they were headed for a blowout. They were comfortably ahead at the end of the second quarter. They were comfortably ahead at the end of the third quarter. And they were still comfortably ahead toward the end of the fourth quarter. In fact, with just forty-two seconds left in the game, Yale led Harvard by sixteen points, 29–13.

But then, Mr. Leigh?

Mr. Leigh: Harvard scored a touchdown (29–19).

Prof. Barry: And?

Mr. Leigh: Got a two-point conversion (29–21).

Prof. Barry: Which led to?

Mr. Leigh: An onside kick (29–21).

Prof. Barry: Followed by?

Mr. Leigh: Another touchdown (29–27).

Prof. Barry: To which Harvard added?

Mr. Leigh: Another two-point conversion (29–29).

Prof. Barry: Which means?

Mr. Leigh: In just forty-two seconds . . .

Prof. Barry: The time it usually takes to run just one or two plays.

Mr. Leigh: Harvard scored sixteen points and tied the score.

Prof. Barry: Which is how the game ended in a tie.

Mr. Leigh: Right.

Prof. Barry: For those of you who know about "The Drive" by John Elway, or "The Catch" by Dwight Clark, or "The Immaculate Reception" by Franco Harris, this Harvard comeback was like all those plays combined. It really was incredible.

Mr. Leigh: Yeah. Watching it in the documentary was crazy. I can't imagine what it must have been like to actually be at the game.

Prof. Barry: Well, that's kind of what I want everybody to do now. I want you all to imagine you were covering the game for Harvard's school newspaper, the *Harvard Crimson*. Focus in particular on the headline you would choose.

Mr. Leigh: Just the headline?

Prof. Barry: Just the headline. Remember what we learned before about *audience*. Remember what we learned about *function*. Remember how what might be a "bitter defeat" to one team and its fans is most likely a "thrilling victory" to the other team and its fans. Remember, most of all, what we keep stressing: the words you choose can change the world people see.

17

Stuns

Prof. Barry: Ms. Ida, please start us off. What did you come up with for the *Harvard Crimson* headline?

Ms. Ida: "Harvard Stuns Yale with Thrilling Fourth Quarter Comeback."

Prof. Barry: Wonderful. Talk us through your choices there.

Ms. Ida: Well, I wanted to focus on the end of the game.

Prof. Barry: Why?

Ms. Ida: Because for readers of the *Harvard Crimson*, that was the most exciting part. It must have been really fun to watch their team come from behind like that.

Prof. Barry: Yet for the readers of the *Yale Daily News*?

Ms. Ida: Not so fun.

Prof. Barry: For those readers, you wouldn't use the word "comeback," would you? Instead, you'd use?

Ms. Ida: Probably something more like "collapse."

Prof. Barry: Like that *USA Today* article from before, about the US meltdown at the Ryder Cup.

Ms. Ida: Right.

Prof. Barry: And how about that great verb your headline uses, "stuns"? Why did you go with "Harvard Stuns Yale" rather than, for example, "Harvard Surprises Yale" or "Harvard Astonishes Yale"?

Ms. Ida: I was looking for a short, powerful verb.

Prof. Barry: Good. With headlines, there seems to be a premium on punchiness.

Ms. Ida: Right.

Prof. Barry: And neither "surprises" nor "astonishes" is that.

Ms. Ida: Not really, no.

Prof. Barry: Plus, those words certainly don't convey the dazing effect I imagine Harvard's comeback had on Yale. "Surprises" is too light and neutral. And "astonishes" is too pretentious and cumbersome.

Ms. Ida: Yeah.

Prof. Barry: I suppose you could have gone with "Harvard Shocks Yale."

Ms. Ida: I thought about that.

Prof. Barry: But?

Ms. Ida: "S-h-o-c-k-s" is a slightly longer word than "S-t-u-n-s." I was trying to keep the headline as short as possible.

Prof. Barry: Smart move. Your copyeditor will appreciate your parsimony.

18

Preserves

Prof. Barry: Who else is willing to share their headline—maybe you, Ms. Henrietta?

Ms. Henrietta: Sure.

Prof. Barry: What did you go with?

Ms. Henrietta: I went with "Thrilling Fourth Quarter Rally Preserves Undefeated Season."

Prof. Barry: Nice—especially the last few words: "Preserves Undefeated Season." Why do you think I singled those out?

Ms. Henrietta: Maybe because it makes a bigger-picture victory out of a smaller-picture nonvictory?

Prof. Barry: Exactly. By coming back to tie the score 29–29, Harvard certainly didn't win the game. But they also didn't?

Ms. Henrietta: Lose the game.

Prof. Barry: Which means?

Ms. Henrietta: Their undefeated record, something they had worked hard all season to earn, was still intact.

Prof. Barry: Good. Now explain how your headline is sort of like the second *Detroit Free Press* headline we talked about, the one that went with "Hail, Hail to the NCAA Runner-Up" right after Michigan lost in the 2013 Final Four.

Ms. Henrietta: I guess both headlines take an outcome that wasn't technically a win and put it in a context that reframes it as something worth celebrating.

Prof. Barry: Do you think, after that game, Harvard students actually celebrated?

Ms. Henrietta: Probably.

Prof. Barry: Do you think they felt like they won?

Ms. Henrietta: Yeah. I kind of do.

Prof. Barry: Well, you're not alone. The editors of the *Harvard Crimson* that year came to the same conclusion. Here's the headline they chose for the next day's paper. Would you mind reading it for us, Ms. Henrietta? It's the title of the documentary Mr. Leigh watched.

HARVARD BEATS YALE, 29-29

The Harvard Crimson

Champi's Passing Quiets Yale Fans

Ms. Henrietta: "Harvard Beats Yale, 29–29."

Prof. Barry: Pretty clever, right?

Ms. Henrietta: Yeah.

Prof. Barry: It's also a great example of those definitions of "good writing" we started class with. Let's start with the first definition. Read it again, please.

Ms. Henrietta: "Good writing is the best words in their best order."

Prof. Barry: How might this first definition apply to "Harvard Beats Yale, 29–29"? How is "Harvard Beats Yale, 29–29" the "best words in their best order"?

Ms. Henrietta: Maybe because . . .

Prof. Barry: Or, actually, just focus on the first part of that definition for now. What makes "Harvard Beats Yale, 29–29" the "best words" to describe what happened in this football game, at least from the perspective of Harvard fans?

Ms. Henrietta: For one thing, "Harvard Beats Yale, 29–29" is pretty simple and straightforward.

Prof. Barry: Yet it is also?

Ms. Henrietta: Really funny and imaginative.

Prof. Barry: Good. In a very tiny space, those words create an entirely new way to think about the outcome of that game. And while the wording is unexpected—especially "Beats"—don't they seem, in some sense, inevitable, at least once you read them?

I mean, I would *never* have created "Harvard Beats Yale, 29–29" on my own. But once I saw it, I thought, "Yes, of course. Of course that's the headline. No other headline would do."

Ms. Henrietta: Right.

Prof. Barry: And how about the second part of the definition, the part about finding not just the "best words" but also "the best words in their best order"? Suppose the editors had kept the same words but rearranged the order. Suppose the headline read "29–29, Harvard Beats Yale."

Ms. Henrietta: That'd be weird.

Prof. Barry: And a bit confusing, right?

Ms. Henrietta: Yeah. I might think it was a typo.

Prof. Barry: Exactly. The score has to come at the end, after "Harvard Beats Yale." You can't have "29–29" appear first. You'd ruin the headline's surprise.

Ms. Henrietta: Right.

Prof. Barry: Of course, "the best words in their best order" is just one of the three definitions of good writing we talked about. Please remind us of the second, Ms. Henrietta.

Ms. Henrietta: "Good writing is getting something right in language."

Prof. Barry: And how is "Harvard Beats Yale, 29–29" an example of that? How is it an example of "getting something right in language"?

Ms. Henrietta: I think it's sort of like what I said before. After such an amazing fourth-quarter comeback, Harvard fans probably felt like they won the game. They probably felt like they had beaten Yale, even though the scoreboard showed a tie.

Prof. Barry: What we get from the scoreboard is in some ways merely data, right?

Ms. Henrietta: Right.

Prof. Barry: Yet from the headline "Harvard Beats Yale, 29–29," we get more of a story, more of an emotion, more of a complete sense of how the game was experienced.

Ms. Henrietta: Definitely.

Prof. Barry: Don't get me wrong: I love data. I love big data, I love small data, I'd love petite data—if there were such a thing.

But I also think that you are on to something, Ms. Henrietta, when you suggest that by giving us more than just the tie score, the editors of the *Harvard Crimson* provide a better sense of how the game was experienced—both by the players and by the fans.

If the editors had given us just the point total without any framing language, readers wouldn't necessarily know how incredible the event was. They wouldn't know that this tie wasn't a standard tie—that, for Harvard, it wasn't a neutral outcome at all. Instead, it was, as we have been saying, pretty much a win.

19

Order Out of Chaos

Prof. Barry: Okay. At this point, we have seen how the definition "the best words in their best order" applies to "Harvard Beats Yale, 29–29," and we have seen how the definition "getting something right in language" applies to "Harvard Beats Yale, 29–29." So finish off the list for us, Ms. Henrietta. What was our third definition of good writing?

Ms. Henrietta: "Good writing is making order out of chaos."

Prof. Barry: Now apply that to "Harvard Beats Yale, 29–29." How did the editors of the *Harvard Crimson* make order out of chaos when they came up with that headline?

Ms. Henrietta: Well, you said it was a pretty crazy game.

Prof. Barry: Right.

Ms. Henrietta: And maybe even a chaotic one, at least at the end.

Prof. Barry: Definitely.

Ms. Henrietta: So what I think the headline does is impose some order on that chaos. It gives a tidy, matter-of-fact way to sum up the game: "Harvard Beats Yale, 29–29."

Prof. Barry: Good. Imagine what it must have been like when the game finally ended. People probably went home thinking, *My goodness. What just happened?*

Ms. Henrietta: Yeah.

Prof. Barry: But then, the next morning, everyone opens up the *Harvard Crimson*, looks at the headline, reads "Harvard Beats Yale, 29–29," and realizes, "Oh yeah. *That's* what happened."

What seemed like chaos has now, wonderfully, been given a helpful bit of order.

20

Poetry

Prof. Barry: So we have these three helpful definitions of good writing, Mr. Wild. We have "the best words in their best order." We have "getting something right in language." And we have "making order out of chaos."

Mr. Wild: Right.

Prof. Barry: The question is, Who came up with them?

Mr. Wild: Okay.

Prof. Barry: I ask you because you are our English major, and I'm hoping you might have some guesses, particularly for the first one: good writing is "the best words in the best order." That's the most famous.

Mr. Wild: It sounds really familiar.

Prof. Barry: "The best words in their best order"?

Mr. Wild: Yeah. Was it a Romantic poet?

Prof. Barry: It was.

Mr. Wild: John Keats?

Prof. Barry: Close.

Mr. Wild: William Wordsworth?

Prof. Barry: Closer.

Mr. Wild: Samuel Taylor Coleridge?

Prof. Barry: Yup. The Romantic poet Samuel Taylor Coleridge came up with the phrase "the best words in their best order." But he wasn't defining good writing exactly, or at least he wasn't defining good writing in general. Instead, he was defining a specific kind of good writing. Do you know which kind?

Mr. Wild: Poetry?

Prof. Barry: Good. When Coleridge used the phrase "the best words in their best order," he was defining what he meant by "poetry."

Mr. Wild: Poetry is "the best words in their best order."

Prof. Barry: Exactly. It's a nice little definition, don't you think?

Mr. Wild: Yeah.

Prof. Barry: And it's actually not the only definition of poetry on our list. The person behind our second definition of good writing—"getting something right in language"—was also defining what he meant by "poetry."

Do you know who that person is, Mr. Wild? Do you know who defined poetry as "getting something right in language"? He's another poet.

Mr. Wild: I don't think so.

Prof. Barry: You ever heard of a guy named Howard Nemerov? He put that definition of poetry in the second line of an essay called "Poetry and Meaning" published back in 1973.

Mr. Wild: What did he write in the first line?

Prof. Barry: "What I have to say to you is very simple—so simple that I find it hard to say."

Mr. Wild: Wait, I think I actually *have* heard of this guy.

Prof. Barry: Yeah?

Mr. Wild: Yeah. I never would have guessed his name, and I certainly haven't read that essay. But I'm pretty sure we looked at one of his poems in a class I took on war poetry.

Prof. Barry: Did the poem involve fighter jets?

Mr. Wild: Yeah. It's really sad.

Prof. Barry: Might have been "The War in the Air." Nemerov was a pilot in World War II.

Mr. Wild: That's what my teacher said.

Prof. Barry: It's great that you've heard of him. His poems really are worth revisiting. Of course, if any of you haven't heard of him, even better. Now you can have the treat of reading the words of a great writer you didn't even know existed.

21

Most Distilled and Most Powerful

Prof. Barry: So we have learned, Mr. Wild, that the phrase "the best words in their best order" comes from?

Mr. Wild: Samuel Taylor Coleridge.

Prof. Barry: And we have learned that the phrase "getting something right in language" comes from?

Mr. Wild: Howard Nemerov.

Prof. Barry: That means we only have one phrase to go. Remind us what it is, please.

Mr. Wild: "Making order out of chaos."

Prof. Barry: Any guess who's responsible for that one? I'll give you a hint: it's going to be hard to be wrong.

Mr. Wild: What do you mean?

Prof. Barry: I mean you could say the name of virtually any poet, and you'd probably be right. You could also say the name of virtually any painter, or composer, or computer programmer. Any designer, sculptor, or carpenter. Any lawyer. Any engineer. Any comedian. Any historian. Any *parent*.

People in all of these positions—and many more like them—have at some point probably told someone or perhaps just thought to themselves, *You know, what I do each day with my pen (or my chisel, or these lines of codes, or these toddlers) is make order out of chaos. I take something that, even as recently as this morning, lacked form, and I give it form. I take something that desperately needed structure, and I give it structure. I take something that had no coherence, no organization, no concrete life, and I give it all those things—and then I add in a little bit of my own style and personality too.*

Mr. Wild: So you're saying that the phrase could have come from anybody?

Prof. Barry: I don't know about *anybody*. But it is certainly a thought many people have had. Here, for example, is a passage from Edwidge Danticat's wonderful short story collection *Krik? Krak!* that expresses this idea of making order out of chaos.

Mr. Wild: "When you write, it's like braiding your hair. Taking a handful of coarse unruly strands and attempting to bring them into unity."

Prof. Barry: And here's the poet Rafael Campo—who also happens to be a doctor—making a similar point, although this time on a much more personal level.

Mr. Wild: "I knew at an early age that I was gay, and so poetry has also been a place to heal the wound of being made, by society, to feel so painfully that difference. The poem, I've always felt, is an opportunity for me to create an integrated whole from so many broken shards."

Prof. Barry: Or how about this from Justice Oliver Wendell Holmes, one of the greatest writers ever to sit on the Supreme Court?

Mr. Wild: "The mark of a master is, that facts which before lay scattered in an inorganic mass, when he shoots through them the magnetic current of his thought, leap into an organic order, and live and bear fruit."

Prof. Barry: But perhaps the most direct statement comes from a slide the documentary filmmaker Ken Burns uses in his examination of legendary architect Frank Lloyd Wright. As Burns transitions between Wright's childhood and his adult years, the screen goes black, and the following stark, white letters appear.

Mr. Wild: "Order Out of Chaos."

Prof. Barry: Pretty simple and straightforward, huh?

Mr. Wild: Yeah.

Prof. Barry: But even if people from many backgrounds and disciplines think in those terms, focus for now on the poetic approach to making order out of chaos—not in the sense of producing a sonnet or a sestina or even knowing the difference between those two things. I don't think I care whether you ever do.

What I care about is that you develop the ability to generate, when you need to, language at its most distilled and most powerful, which is how the great Rita Dove defines poetry. It might also be nice if you became a person who is passionately in love with language, which is what W. H. Auden suggests is the most fundamental characteristic of a poet.

To do all this, however, we are going to need some help. From a French dude.

22
Flaubert

Prof. Barry: Anyone in here speak French?

Ms. Warsaw: I do.

Prof. Barry: Is that your major—French?

Ms. Warsaw: No. Physics.

Prof. Barry: Physics?

Ms. Warsaw: And chemistry.

Prof. Barry: Physics and chemistry? You're majoring in physics and chemistry? And you speak French?

Ms. Warsaw: Yup.

Prof. Barry: Do you speak any other languages?

Ms. Warsaw: Besides English?

Prof. Barry: Yeah.

Ms. Warsaw: I grew up speaking Russian in school.

Prof. Barry: Geez. Well, maybe we'll find some use for your Russian later in the semester. For now, we'll just need your French. You ever hear of Gustave Flaubert?

Ms. Warsaw: Yeah.

Prof. Barry: What do you know about him?

Ms. Warsaw: He's French.

Prof. Barry: Yup.

Ms. Warsaw: He was a writer.

Prof. Barry: Yup.

Ms. Warsaw: And he was very precise.

Prof. Barry: About?

Ms. Warsaw: Language.

Prof. Barry: That's true. He was fantastically, even fastidiously, precise about language—including punctuation. He supposedly once wrote the following. Read it for us, please.

Ms. Warsaw: "I spent the morning putting in a comma . . ."

Prof. Barry: Keep going.

Ms. Warsaw: ". . . and the afternoon removing it."

Prof. Barry: Pretty good, huh?

Ms. Warsaw: Yeah.

Prof. Barry: Like a lot of great quotes, that one has been attributed to many different people, including Oscar Wilde. But whoever said it, the sentiment is a good reminder of the thought and deliberateness that we will be shooting for in our writing, as is a fun anecdote about Flaubert that I want to share. I'll need your French skills to do that.

23

Le Mot Juste

Prof. Barry: The anecdote has a few variations, but I'll focus on a version that centers on a night early in Flaubert's career when a friend of his stopped by to check on how his writing was going. He said, "Hey, Flauby"—That was Flaubert's nickname: "Flauby." Pronounced "Flow-be."

Ms. Warsaw: Really? Flaubert's nickname was "Flauby"?

Prof. Barry: No. Not really. But it would be great if it were.

Ms. Warsaw: Did he even *have* a nickname?

Prof. Barry: Not that I know of. But he did sometimes give other people nicknames. He called Ivan Turgenev, the great Russian novelist, "Poire Molle" for example.

Ms. Warsaw: "Poire Molle"?

Prof. Barry: Yeah. Can you please translate that for us?

Ms. Warsaw: "Soft pear"?

Prof. Barry: That's right. Soft Pear. Not exactly the first image that comes to mind when you think of Russian novelists. But apparently that's what Flaubert called him. They became friends in Paris in 1863 and eventually established quite a letter-writing relationship, one that continued all the way until Flaubert's death in 1880.

Ms. Warsaw: So is Turgenev the friend in the anecdote?

Prof. Barry: No. I don't actually know the name of that friend. I just know that he specifically asked Flaubert how his writing was coming along.

Ms. Warsaw: What did Flaubert say?

Prof. Barry: He said something like, "Very well. My writing has been coming along very well. I have written . . . one word."

Ms. Warsaw: One word?

Prof. Barry: Yeah, one word.

Ms. Warsaw: So what did the friend say to that?

Prof. Barry: What do you think he said?

Ms. Warsaw: Maybe something like, "At least we have moved on to actual words. Yesterday, you were just adding and removing commas."

Prof. Barry: Not quite. But he was pretty confused, particularly at how triumphant Flaubert seemed when announcing that he had only written one word.

Ms. Warsaw: The friend didn't think that was very impressive?

Prof. Barry: No. Not for a whole day's work. "You really only wrote one word?" he asked. "All this time, twelve hours, and you didn't even write a full page, a full paragraph, a full sentence? Isn't that a little disappointing, even depressing?"

Mr. Warsaw: What did Flaubert say?

Prof. Barry: "No. It is not disappointing. It is not depressing."

Ms. Warsaw: Did Flaubert say why?

Prof. Barry: He did. "Yes, I only wrote one word today," he said, "but—." And then Flaubert paused, smiled, and said something we are going to need your help translating.

Ms. Warsaw: Okay.

Prof. Barry: He said, "That word was—*le mot juste*."

Ms. Warsaw: That's pretty great.

Prof. Barry: Isn't it? Now translate it for us, please, so everyone else can know what you mean.

Ms. Warsaw: He said, "Yes, I only wrote one word today, but that word was—*the right word*."

24
Second Cousin

Prof. Barry: The reliability of that story is a little questionable. But even if it isn't true, it should be, particularly because Flaubert became known for this idea of *le mot juste*. He would work for hours, days, even weeks to find the best way to phrase things.

You're not necessarily going to have that kind of time when writing here at Michigan or when you start your careers. But I hope you are at least starting to understand how important it is to choose your words with care and purpose.

Mark Twain actually has a nice way of capturing this point. Want to read it for us, Ms. Toth? I saw on your résumé that you're a big fan of his.

Ms. Toth: Sure.

Prof. Barry: Here it is.

Ms. Toth: "Use the right word, not its second cousin."

Prof. Barry: Recognize where that comes from?

Ms. Toth: *Huck Finn*?

Prof. Barry: Nope.

Ms. Toth: *Tom Sawyer*?

Prof. Barry: Nope. It's not from any of his works of fiction.

Ms. Toth: Then I might not know it. I've mostly read his novels and short stories.

Prof. Barry: Yeah, this piece is a lot lesser known. It is a pretty harsh essay that Twain published about James Fenimore Cooper, the guy who wrote *The Last of the Mohicans*. Twain wasn't a fan.

Ms. Toth: Of *The Last of the Mohicans*?

Prof. Barry: Actually, I don't know what Twain thought of *The Last of the Mohicans*. The essay focused on Cooper's writing style in general and two other stories in particular: *The Pathfinder* and *The Deerslayer*. Twain said the following about *The Deerslayer*.

Ms. Toth: "In one place in 'Deerslayer,' and in the restricted space of two-thirds of a page, Cooper has scored 114 offenses against literary art out of a possible 115."

Prof. Barry: Kind of makes you wonder what the 115th offense might have been.

Ms. Toth: Yeah.

Prof. Barry: Maybe someone can look it up after class—though I am pretty sure Twain was being facetious. He wrote similarly satirical, borderline mean things about Jane Austen, about Robert Louis Stevenson, about . . .

Ms. Toth: Is Twain the one who described a bunch of female writers as a "damned mob of scribbling women"?

Prof. Barry: No. That was Nathaniel Hawthorne, another author whose style Twain didn't really like. But what Twain did like was, as I said, finding the right word. Here's another observation he once made about the importance of doing that.

Ms. Toth: "The difference between the almost right word and the right word is really a large matter—'tis the difference between the lightning bug and the lightning."

Prof. Barry: Pretty clever, huh?

Ms. Toth: Yeah.

Prof. Barry: Some really wonderful law students gave me a card once with that quote in it.

Ms. Toth: Were they Twain fans?

Prof. Barry: I'm not sure. But they really came to appreciate the difference between the right word and the almost right word. To further illustrate this difference, I now want to tell you all a story. In fact, I want to tell you two stories. Each is about a famous sports figure who was, at various points and by various people, called "Bobby."

As we'll see, however, with one of them, "Bobby" was often the right word. But with the other, it was, rather painfully, only *almost* the right word.

25

A Tale of Two Bobbys

Prof. Barry: Would you be up for helping me tell the first story, Ms. Bristol? I need someone who knows something about Bobby Knight. Based on your answers so far in class, I am guessing you do.

Ms. Bristol: Sure. I know who Bobby Knight is.

Prof. Barry: Great. Who is he? What is he known for?

Ms. Bristol: Coaching basketball. Throwing chairs. Sometimes doing both at the same time.

Prof. Barry: That's true, unfortunately. The chair-throwing, for many people, tends to overshadow his on-court and off-court accomplishments. Do you know any of those?

Ms. Bristol: Didn't he win something like nine hundred games as a coach?

Prof. Barry: He did. It was the most all-time among men's basketball coaches in college when he retired in 2008.

Ms. Bristol: He also won four national championships.

Prof. Barry: Yup—but not all as a coach. He also won one as a player.

Ms. Bristol: Really? I didn't know he won one as a player. With which team?

Prof. Barry: You're not going to like this answer. No self-respecting Michigan student will.

Ms. Bristol: What is it—Michigan State?

Prof. Barry: Worse.

Ms. Bristol: Ohio State?

Prof. Barry: Yup. He won the 1961 NCAA championship with Ohio State. He was on a team with future NBA Hall-of-Famers John Havlicek and Jerry Lucas. Of course, Knight's a lot better known for his coaching than he is for his playing. You remember where he did most of that coaching?

Ms. Bristol: Indiana University.

Prof. Barry: Did he ever get sanctioned by the NCAA for recruiting violations?

Ms. Bristol: Not that I know of.

Prof. Barry: Did most of his students graduate?

Ms. Bristol: I think something like 98 percent, at least at Indiana.

Prof. Barry: Did he coach anywhere else?

Ms. Bristol: Didn't he start out at West Point?

Prof. Barry: Yeah. Soon after graduating from Ohio State, Knight enlisted in the Army and was named assistant coach of the basketball team at West Point, the military academy where Army officers are educated and trained. Then, two years later, at the age of only twenty-four, he was named the head coach.

Ms. Bristol: Is that how he got the nickname "The General"? Because he coached at West Point?

Prof. Barry: Yup. And you know who one of his players was at West Point?

Ms. Bristol: Who?

Prof. Barry: The coach who eventually broke Knight's collegiate win record.

Ms. Bristol: Dean Smith? At North Carolina?

Prof. Barry: No. That's whose record Knight broke. Think North Carolina's biggest rival.

Ms. Bristol: Duke?

Prof. Barry: Yeah. Who's their legendary coach?

Ms. Bristol: Coach K, Mike Krzyzewski.

Prof. Barry: Right.

Ms. Bristol: Are you serious? Bobby Knight once coached Coach K?

Prof. Barry: He did. And then they actually coached together for a little while. In 1974, after being discharged from active duty in the Army, Coach K became one of Knight's assistant coaches at Indiana.

Ms. Bristol: Coach K as "Assistant Coach K." Weird.

Prof. Barry: I know. Perhaps even weirder is that Coach K actually went back to West Point to be the head coach. Which means two of the winningest basketball coaches of all time both got their start leading teams not just of star athletes but of future soldiers.

26

Hey, Knight, What's Up?

Prof. Barry: So Bobby Knight starts out at West Point, Ms. Bristol, and then he coaches for about three decades at Indiana.

Ms. Bristol: Right.

Prof. Barry: Why did he stop coaching at Indiana? Why did he move to—what was the school?

Ms. Bristol: Texas Tech.

Prof. Barry: Yeah, why did he move to Texas Tech? Wasn't he a legend at Indiana, right along with his iconic red sweater?

Ms. Bristol: He left because he was forced to leave.

Prof. Barry: And why was he forced to leave?

Ms. Bristol: Because of an incident.

Prof. Barry: What kind of an incident?

Ms. Bristol: An incident that followed a whole bunch of other incidents.

Prof. Barry: Like?

Ms. Bristol: The chair throwing.

Prof. Barry: And?

Ms. Bristol: A former player claiming Knight choked him during a practice.

Prof. Barry: And?

Ms. Bristol: I don't remember all the details of the other incidents. All I remember is that after the choking allegations, which came out in, I think, the spring of 2000, the president of Indiana, Myles Brand . . .

Prof. Barry: Who would eventually become the president of the NCAA.

Ms. Bristol: Yeah, that guy. He put Knight on a "zero tolerance" policy.

Prof. Barry: Which meant?

Ms. Bristol: If there was another incident, Knight would be fired.

Prof. Barry: And so?

Ms. Bristol: There was another incident.

Prof. Barry: When?

Ms. Bristol: In the fall of that year.

Prof. Barry: Involving?

Ms. Bristol: A first-year student.

Prof. Barry: A basketball player?

Ms. Bristol: No. He wasn't an athlete. He was a regular student.

Prof. Barry: What happened?

Ms. Bristol: I don't know for sure, but the story is that the student went to pick up tickets from the basketball arena. Then, as the student was leaving the ticket office and heading outside, he saw Knight.

Prof. Barry: Did the student wave?

Ms. Bristol: Not exactly.

Prof. Barry: Did he smile and keep walking?

Ms. Bristol: No.

Prof. Barry: What did he do?

Ms. Bristol: He said something like, "Hey, Knight, what's up?"

Prof. Barry: That's it?

Ms. Bristol: That's it.

Prof. Barry: How did Knight respond?

Ms. Bristol: Not well.

Prof. Barry: He didn't say "Not much, first-year student. How 'bout you?"

Ms. Bristol: No.

Prof. Barry: He didn't give him a high-five?

Ms. Bristol: No.

Prof. Barry: A fist bump?

Ms. Bristol: No.

Prof. Barry: What did he do?

Ms. Bristol: He grabbed the student.

Prof. Barry: Hard?

Ms. Bristol: According to the student, yeah. He claimed Knight left marks on his arm. But according to Mike Davis, the assistant coach who witnessed the incident, the whole exchange was pretty mild mannered. Knight never cursed. He never even raised his voice.

Prof. Barry: But Knight definitely wasn't pleased.

Ms. Bristol: Right. He definitely wasn't pleased. He allegedly told the kid, "Son, my name is not 'Knight' to you. I don't call people by their last name, and neither should you."

Prof. Barry: Kind of reinforces the theme of today's class, doesn't it? The words you choose can change the world people see.

Or modified slightly: the *names* you choose can change the world people see. Because what did Bobby Knight see, Ms. Bristol, when the student decided to refer to him as "Knight"?

Ms. Bristol: A sign of disrespect.

Prof. Barry: Yet if the student had simply put a "Coach" or "Mr." in front of that "Knight," who knows . . .

Ms. Bristol: Perhaps Bobby Knight would still be coaching at Indiana.

Prof. Barry: I'm not sure I would go that far. Myles Brand, the president who ousted Knight, had a whole list of grievances against Knight. But this first part of our "Tale of Two Bobbys" is certainly another reminder of how, even in passing and especially when it comes to somebody's name, your choice of words can have powerful, even devastating consequences.

Yet here's a question, Ms. Bristol: Is it a sign of disrespect that you and I have been, at times, referring to Coach Bobby Knight as just "Knight"?

Ms. Bristol: What do you mean?

Prof. Barry: I mean that when I earlier mentioned Duke's Mike Krzyzewski—or "Coach K"—I didn't describe him as "the coach who eventually broke *Mr.* Knight's collegiate win record." Nor did I describe him as "the coach who eventually broke *Coach* Knight's collegiate win record."

Instead, I described him as "the coach who eventually broke Knight's collegiate win record."

Ms. Bristol: Right.

Prof. Barry: And when you were recalling the encounter at the ticket office, you said that as the students was leaving and heading outside, "he saw Knight." You didn't say "he saw Mr. Knight." You didn't say "he saw Coach Knight." You just said "he saw Knight."

Ms. Bristol: I don't know.

Prof. Barry: What don't you know?

Ms. Bristol: I don't know if it's the same.

Prof. Barry: Why?

Ms. Bristol: Because tons of people refer to Bobby Knight as "Knight." On television, at bars, in magazines and books.

Prof. Barry: To his face?

Ms. Bristol: No.

Prof. Barry: Could that be an important difference?

Ms. Bristol: Maybe. I guess it's different when you're addressing someone directly.

Prof. Barry: So it's an "audience" issue?

Ms. Bristol: Yeah. You talk to people in a much different way than you talk about them. It's like with teachers.

Prof. Barry: Teachers?

Ms. Bristol: Yeah. I refer to my teachers by their last names all the time, but only when I'm talking to a friend or something. If I saw one of those teachers—or, let's say you, Professor Barry. If I saw you walking across the Diag or coming out of the Big House, there would be no way I'd say, "Hey, Barry, what's up?"

Prof. Barry: What if I first said to you, "Hey, Bristol, what's up?"

Ms. Bristol: I think I'd start laughing.

Prof. Barry: Later in the class, we'll talk about what I call each of you and why I decided to go with your last names. But right now, let's turn to the second story in our "Tale of Two Bobbys." It's going to show us how disrespect can creep into a name even when the person is not being addressed directly.

27

When God Started Playing Right Field

Prof. Barry: Who's been to Puerto Rico?

Ms. Yona: I have.

Prof. Barry: A lot?

Ms. Yona: Yeah.

Prof. Barry: Have you been to San Juan?

Ms. Yona: Sí.

Prof. Barry: You speak Spanish?

Ms. Yona: Sí. I grew up in Chile.

Prof. Barry: Nice. I asked you about San Juan because there's a stadium there named after a famous Puerto Rican baseball player. Do you know it?

Ms. Yona: I think so. The one named after Clemente, right?

Prof. Barry: Right. Do you know Clemente's full name?

Ms. Yona: Roberto Clemente Walker.

Prof. Barry: Good. You even got the order of his name right.

Ms. Yona: What do you mean?

Prof. Barry: Well, when Clemente's plaque first went up at the Baseball Hall of Fame in Cooperstown, it read "Robert Walker Clemente." You know why?

Ms. Yona: Because the person who made the plaque wasn't Puerto Rican.

Prof. Barry: Exactly. But explain what you mean.

Ms. Yona: "Clemente" was the last name of Roberto Clemente's father. "Walker" was the maiden name of his mother. And in Puerto Rico, like in many Hispanic parts of the world, the custom is to list your mom's maiden name after your dad's last name.

Prof. Barry: So if President Franklin Delano Roosevelt, the son of James Roosevelt and Sara Ann Delano, had been born and raised in Puerto Rico, his name wouldn't have been "Franklin Delano Roosevelt."

Ms. Yona: Right.

Prof. Barry: Instead, it would have been?

Ms. Yona: Franklin Roosevelt Delano.

Prof. Barry: Exactly. But before I asked that, I should have asked a preliminary question: How the heck did you know Roberto Clemente's mother's maiden name?

Ms. Yona: My grandfather is Puerto Rican. He lives in San Juan. He's the reason I've been there a bunch of times. And he *loves* Roberto Clemente.

Prof. Barry: Yeah?

Ms. Yona: Yeah. It's kind of out of control. His favorite day of the year is April 17.

Prof. Barry: Because that's the day Clemente was born?

Ms. Yona: No. Because that's the day, in 1955, when Clemente debuted for the Pittsburgh Pirates. Or as my grandfather would say, "Ese es el día cuando Dios comenzó a jugar en jardín derecho."

Prof. Barry: You want to translate that for everybody?

Ms. Yona: "That is the day when God started playing right field."

Prof. Barry: Great. Thank you.

Ms. Yona: Because of my grandfather, I know how many all-star games Clemente played in.

Prof. Barry: How many?

Ms. Yona: Fifteen. I also know how many Gold Gloves he won.

Prof. Barry: How many?

Ms. Yona: Twelve.

Prof. Barry: That ties him with Willie Mays. The two of them share the record for Gold Gloves won by an outfielder.

Ms. Yona: I even know that Clemente finished his career with three thousand hits, that his lifetime batting average was .317, and that he was inducted into the Hall of Fame, through a special vote, only about six months after he played his final game.

Prof. Barry: You want to tell everyone why that last part is unusual?

Ms. Yona: About the Hall of Fame?

Prof. Barry: Yeah. What's weird about Clemente getting voted in only about six months after he played his last game?

Ms. Yona: Baseball players generally have to wait at least five years before they even go on the ballot.

Prof. Barry: So why the special vote for Clemente?

Ms. Yona: Because of the way he died.

Prof. Barry: Which was?

Ms. Yona: In a plane crash.

Prof. Barry: Going where?

Ms. Yona: Nicaragua.

Prof. Barry: And why was he going to Nicaragua?

Ms. Yona: It was a humanitarian trip. There was a massive earthquake in Managua, the capital city of Nicaragua, right around Christmas in 1972. Clemente was bringing relief supplies.

Prof. Barry: Why didn't he just arrange for the supplies to be sent without him? Why did he insist on going himself?

Ms. Yona: He did arrange for the supplies to be sent without him, initially. But then people told him that the supplies were being snagged by corrupt officials.

Prof. Barry: So what did Clemente do?

Ms. Yona: He chartered a plane—an old plane, unfortunately, a really old plane.

Prof. Barry: He figured that by showing up in person, by delivering the supplies himself, the supplies would more likely make it to the people who needed them.

Ms. Yona: Yeah. When you want a job done right . . .

Prof. Barry: Send Clemente.

28

Jose DiMaggio

Prof. Barry: To commemorate Clemente's life and playing career, Major League Baseball gives out an award every year to the player who best exemplifies the game of baseball, sportsmanship, community involvement, and—there's one other quality.

Ms. Yona: Kindness?

Prof. Barry: Essentially, yeah. But a little more specific.

Ms. Yona: Compassion?

Prof. Barry: I think the phrase is "individual contribution to his team."

Ms. Yona: So being a team player?

Prof. Barry: Yeah. You remember Willie Mays? The player I mentioned who shares the record for Gold Gloves with Clemente?

Ms. Yona: Yeah.

Prof. Barry: He was the first person to win the award back when it was called the Commissioner's Award.

Ms. Yona: Then they changed it to the Clemente Award?

Prof. Barry: Yup. Soon after Clemente died.

Ms. Yona: That makes sense. To people like my grandfather, Clemente was much more than just a baseball player. He was a cultural hero.

Prof. Barry: Do you want to explain a little more why that's the case?

Ms. Yona: Because Clemente was Latino at a time when that wasn't something Major League Baseball players were.

Prof. Barry: That's right. Clemente played in an era before Rod Carew and Pedro Martinez, an era before Mariano Rivera and Albert Pujols, an era before Big Papi!

Ms. Yona: Right.

Prof. Barry: Which helps explain the key to the second part of our "A Tale of Two Bobbys." Do you know what many American commentators at the time called Clemente? Here's a hint: it wasn't "Roberto."

Ms. Yona: Yeah. I know what they called him. It really pissed off my grandfather.

Prof. Barry: What was it?

Ms. Yona: "Bobby." They called him "Bobby Clemente."

Prof. Barry: Or sometimes "Bob." Pick a year. Pretty much any year during Clemente's prime: 1962, 1964, 1966. Then go on eBay and search for his Topps baseball card. You won't find many, I don't think, with the name "Roberto Clemente." Mostly you'll find, over and over again, "Bob Clemente."

Ms. Yona: I know. It's terrible. In protest, my grandfather said he started referring to Joe DiMaggio as "Jose DiMaggio."

Prof. Barry: Really?

Ms. Yona: Yeah. To this day, he'll get really upset and offended when someone refers to Clemente as "Bob" or "Bobby."

Prof. Barry: It wasn't just Topps, though. A bunch of Clemente's teammates called him "Bob" or "Bobby." The *New York Times* called him "Bob" or "Bobby." Even as late as September 30, 1972, when Clemente became just the eleventh player in history, up to that point, to reach three thousand hits, the Pittsburgh Pirates own radio play-by-play announcer called him "Bobby"—once when Clemente was stepping up to the plate and then again as he was rounding first on his way to second base. You can find the clip on YouTube and listen for yourself.

Ms. Yona: Don't tell my grandfather.

Prof. Barry: And remember: this was in 1972 after several more Latino players, like Juan Marichal and Mateo Alou, had joined the league and started doing really well.

It was also after a bunch of other major political and cultural breakthroughs for Latinos in general. In 1954, the Supreme Court held that Mexican Americans were entitled to equal protection under the Constitution in a case called *Hernandez v. Texas*, which is sometimes referred to as the "Hispanic *Brown v. Board of Education*." In the 1960s, labor leader Cesar Chavez generated national support for the rights of farmworkers. And throughout this era, a string of Hispanic actors won Academy Awards—José Ferrer for *Cyrano de Bergerac*, Anthony Quinn for both *Viva Zapata!* and *Lust for Life*, and Rita Moreno for *West Side Story*.

Yet what American announcers did with Roberto Clemente's name erased all of that, or at least obscured it. They covered over his Latino heritage, almost like forcing him to wear white makeup.

That might be a bit of a stretch, but perhaps you can still try to make the connection for us. Particularly for folks like your grandfather, how is calling Clemente "Bob" or "Bobby" instead of "Roberto" sort of like covering his skin with makeup?

Ms. Yona: Because "Bobby" gives Clemente a different complexion. It doesn't announce, the way "Roberto" does, Clemente's ethnic identity.

Prof. Barry: So when your grandfather heard "Roberto," he heard what?

Ms. Yona: He heard his own Puerto Rican heritage. He heard sugarcane. He heard *mofongo*. He heard Three Kings' Day. He heard . . . *himself.*

Prof. Barry: And when he heard "Bobby"?

Ms. Yona: He heard all that get wiped away.

Prof. Barry: Like linguistic vanishing cream.

Ms. Yona: Yeah. Like linguistic vanishing cream.

Prof. Barry: The words you choose, we have been saying . . .

Ms. Yona: Can change the world people see.

Prof. Barry: But not always in a good way.

Ms. Yona: Right.

Prof. Barry: Yet let's be clear: it is not as if Clemente just sat by and accepted all the ignorance and disrespect thrown his way. Did your grandfather ever tell you about the 1971 World Series? Did he tell you about what happened in the locker room, with all the television cameras, after Clemente's team won?

Ms. Yona: He did. He said Clemente looked right into the cameras and—

Prof. Barry: Wait. Let me give some context before you say anything else.

Ms. Yona: Okay.

Prof. Barry: For those of you who don't know, Clemente dominated that World Series. At the age of thirty-seven—so not exactly in the prime of a baseball player's career—he batted .414 over the course of seven games, collected twelve hits, made one of the more amazing throws ever by a right fielder, and smashed the go-ahead home run in the deciding game.

George Will, the writer and big-time baseball aficionado, called Clemente's performance that year one of the greatest in World Series history. I think the exact word Will used was that Clemente's performance was "a jewel."

So it kind of makes sense that Clemente would be interviewed after the game, right?

Ms. Yona: Yeah.

Prof. Barry: And when he was, he took advantage of the opportunity to do something pretty cool, especially to people like your grandfather. What did he do, Ms. Yona, on national television?

Ms. Yona: He spoke in Spanish.

Prof. Barry: Yup. With everybody watching and the camera directly on him, he said, "Before I say anything in English, I want to say something for my mother and father in Spanish." And then he did just that, with a big smile and a whole island's worth of joy.

Ms. Yona: My grandfather said that one gesture filled him with so much pride.

Prof. Barry: It made him feel important?

Ms. Yona: Yeah.

Prof. Barry: It made him feel included?

Ms. Yona: Yeah.

Prof. Barry: Something tells me he wasn't the only one.

29

The Wise Latina

Prof. Barry: I never got to see Clemente play. He died before I was born. But I did get to see, much later, at least a little of the pride Puerto Ricans feel for one another.

Ms. Yona: When?

Prof. Barry: When Sonia Sotomayor became the first Hispanic Supreme Court Justice.

Ms. Yona: Oh yeah, that was big.

Prof. Barry: Huge.

Ms. Yona: "The Wise Latina."

Prof. Barry: Right.

Ms. Yona: My grandfather always calls her "Sonia" as if the two of them are close friends or something. Not "Justice Sotomayor." Not "Sonia Sotomayor." Just "Sonia."

Prof. Barry: That's awesome.

Ms. Yona: My mom too. It's kind of ridiculous. She'll say to me, "You know, we should read Sonia's book, *My Beloved World*." Or "Did you see Sonia on *Sesame Street*? Wasn't she great, chatting up Abby Cadabby?"

Prof. Barry: I think I like your mom.

Ms. Yona: She's crazy. It's as if Sotomayor is our neighbor or something, like she has been over to our house, drank our coffee, sat under our papaya tree—and now just happens to be one of most powerful judges in the world.

Prof. Barry: Justice Sotomayor, who is a big-time baseball fan, visited the law school here at Michigan in 2016. All the faculty members got to meet her. She was extremely warm, gracious, and unpretentious. So I'm guessing she probably wouldn't mind if your mom and grandfather call her "Sonia." She might even prefer it.

But that does raise a question I want to make sure we get to about how this class operates: Why do you think, Ms. Yona, I call you "Ms. Yona"?

30

Homer in Birkenstocks

Prof. Barry: Or I suppose I could ask you, Mr. Marshall. Or you, Ms. Warsaw. Or you, Mr. Dewey. Why do you think I have called every student in this class by their last name?

Mr. Marshall: Because you're a lawyer and that's what you're used to over at the law school.

Prof. Barry: Partly. There has definitely been a tradition of law professors calling students by their last names. But I actually learned it before I joined the law school. In fact, I learned it even before I went to law school myself.

Mr. Dewey (*jumping in*): Did you learn it in college?

Prof. Barry: Yeah.

Mr. Dewey: At the University of Chicago?

Prof. Barry: How did you know I went to Chicago?

Mr. Dewey: I read your faculty bio online. It said you went to college there. And law school.

Prof. Barry: That's right.

Mr. Dewey: I actually grew up near that campus.

Prof. Barry: In Hyde Park?

Mr. Dewey: Yeah. I went to Lab for high school.

Prof. Barry: Nice. Want to explain to everybody what Lab is?

Mr. Dewey: It's a school, kindergarten through twelfth grade, affiliated with the university. The Obama kids went there before the family left Chicago and moved to the White House.

Prof. Barry: Is Lab where you learned about University of Chicago teachers calling students by their last names?

Mr. Dewey: Yeah. When you get to a certain grade level there, you can take classes at the university—up to six, I think.

Prof. Barry: How many did you take?

Mr. Dewey: Three.

Prof. Barry: Any in the humanities?

Mr. Dewey: Yeah.

Prof. Barry: Did you ever have a teacher named James Redfield? When I was there, he taught in the Classics Department and in something called the Committee on Social Thought.

Mr. Dewey: No. But I think a couple of my friends did. He teaches *The Iliad*, right?

Prof. Barry: Yup, he's pretty much Homer. In Birkenstocks.

Mr. Dewey: That's what my friends said. They said he knows essentially the whole poem by heart in English and in Ancient Greek.

Prof. Barry: Did they also mention what it was like to have Redfield call them by their last names—preceded, of course, by a very courteous sounding "Ms." or "Mr."?

Mr. Dewey: Yeah, they said it was pretty cool. And that was my experience too, in other classes.

Prof. Barry: How so?

Mr. Dewey: Well, I was only sixteen when I took my first University of Chicago class.

Prof. Barry: Same with Redfield. He was the son of an anthropologist who taught there, and he had the chance to enroll a couple years earlier than normal. This was back in the 1960s.

Mr. Dewey: Then maybe he felt the way I did.

Prof. Barry: Which was?

Mr. Dewey: Overmatched.

Prof. Barry: Yeah. The University of Chicago can be a bit of an intimidating place. The gothic architecture, the list of Nobel Prize winners, the lurking feeling that the ghost of Milton Friedman is going to ambush you right on the Quad with a Socratic dialogue.

Mr. Dewey: But it actually helped to be called "Mr. Dewey."

Prof. Barry: How come?

Mr. Dewey: It made me feel like what I said in class would be taken seriously, like my comments mattered. It made me feel adult, even though I obviously wasn't.

Prof. Barry: How old were you again?

Mr. Dewey: Sixteen.

Prof. Barry: But the formality made you feel older?

Mr. Dewey: Yeah.

Prof. Barry: And wiser?

Mr. Dewey: A little, yeah.

Prof. Barry: Did you carry that feeling with you when you went back to your regular high school classes?

Mr. Dewey: I don't think so. There, I was just "Freddy" or "Frederick."

Prof. Barry: No "Mr."?

Mr. Dewey: No.

Prof. Barry: No feeling of sophistication?

Mr. Dewey: No.

Prof. Barry: That's a shame. Maybe things would have been different if you went to school in Atlanta.

Mr. Dewey: Atlanta?

Prof. Barry: Yeah, with a teacher named Carolyn Jones. She's featured in a neat book called *Switch* by Stanford's Chip Heath and Duke's Dan Heath, two brothers whose writing I highly recommend. Anybody read one of their books?

Ms. Bart (*jumping in*)**:** I read parts of *Decisive* in one of my business courses. They wrote that, right?

Prof. Barry: Yup. That one is good too. If you take one of my other courses, The Syntax of Slavery, you'll get to talk about it again. We spend some time on its discussion of "confirmation bias," an annoyingly pernicious impediment to good judgment. But in *Switch*—and the example of the teacher Carolyn Turner that the book highlights—the Heath brothers focus on something much more heartwarming: how Turner turned her classroom of first-graders into a place where rambunctious six- and seven-year-olds actually wanted to sit down, be quiet, and learn.

Can you read an excerpt for us, Mr. Dewey? It describes Turner's strategic naming tactic and is part of the reason for my own.

Mr. Dewey: "One of [Jones's] first efforts was to cultivate a culture of learning in her classroom, calling her students 'scholars' and asking them to address each other that way."

Prof. Barry: Read a little more, please.

Mr. Dewey: "When people visited her classroom, she introduced her class as a group of scholars and asked them to define the term for the guest."

Prof. Barry: Now read what the students would say in response—or rather, what they would *shout* in response.

Mr. Dewey: "They would shout, 'A scholar is someone who loves to learn and is good at it!'"

Prof. Barry: Isn't that pretty cool? Carolyn Turner really got these first-graders to embrace being "scholars."

Mr. Dewey: Yeah.

Prof. Barry: She even pushed them to carry that mind-set with them after they left school each day. Read the next part.

Mr. Dewey: "The scholars were encouraged to go home and share what they learned with their families."

Prof. Barry: Can you imagine if your little sisters or brothers came home from school saying they were "scholars" and then excitedly started going through all their newly acquired knowledge? I'd die.

Mr. Dewey: Yeah, it'd be pretty cute—at least for the first few days.

Prof. Barry: Right, I guess it might get a little annoying after a while. But it's still a nice example of someone being purposeful about the way her words and labels can positively affect other people. Here's a final bit from the book. It describes the day Jones knew her "scholars" strategy was working.

Mr. Dewey: "One day, a scholar was called out of the classroom for administrative reasons, and some of the others in the class started groaning. In most classrooms it would have been a groan of jealousy—*Get me out of here, too.* Jones realized, to her surprise, that it was instead a groan of pity. *That kid is going to miss some scholar work*. 'At that moment,' Jones said, 'I knew I had them.'"

31

Verbal Uniform

Mr. Dewey: It sounds like a uniform.

Prof. Barry: What does?

Mr. Dewey: Carolyn Turner calling her first-graders "scholars." It sounds like she's giving them a kind of uniform, something that signals to anyone who visits the class—and to the students themselves—that, one, her first-graders are a team and, two, her first-graders are no ordinary set of first-graders.

Prof. Barry: Yeah, it does. It does sound like she's giving them a uniform. I like that.

Mr. Dewey: Only the uniform's verbal. It's a verbal uniform. Instead of giving them a jersey, a helmet, or a special kind of leotard, she dresses them in language.

Prof. Barry: Which is essentially what I am trying to do when I call of all of you "Ms." or "Mr." or, should it apply, "Mx." I want these words, these ways of being addressed, to trigger a change in you similar to the change that is triggered every time, say, a Michigan football player puts on his shoulder pads and chin strap, or a Michigan softball player grabs her glove.

I want you to get the sense that our classroom is a kind of practice field or arena. In here, you are invited to be a different version of yourself than you are used to being, a version who is more attuned to the nuances of language and the power of careful composition, a version who thinks hard about word choice, word order, and even wordplay—a version, to paraphrase Henry James, on whom nothing is lost.

Mr. Dewey: That makes sense.

Prof. Barry: It's going to take some discipline, some grit. And it will certainly require you to reflect on which writing principles and moves best fit your style, which authors are most worth reading and emulating, and which strengths you'll need to protect against becoming weaknesses. For guidance, we can turn to a bit of advice from a somewhat unexpected place: Hank Aaron.

Ms. Bristol (*jumping in*)**:** The baseball player?

Prof. Barry: Yeah. The baseball player. In an interview back in 2013, forty years after enduring death threats, bomb threats, and racial slur after racial slur on his way to breaking Babe Ruth's record for career home runs, Hank Aaron said the following when asked what lesson he would like young people to learn from his career.

Ms. Bristol: "I want them to understand that there is no shortcut in life. I want them to understand that if you're looking for short-cuts, then life is not going to treat you very well."

Prof. Barry: Not bad, huh? It's sort of like the oft-repeated advice from the painter and photographer Chuck Close, addressing the juvenile way some folks celebrate "inspiration." Stephen King uses a version of this advice in his book *On Writing*. Philip Roth uses a version of it in his novel *Everyman*. And so does pretty much every book on creativity ever. You want to read it for us?

Ms. Bristol: "Inspiration is for amateurs. The rest of us just show up and get to work."

Prof. Barry: Along these same lines is one of my favorite bits of wisdom, partly because the person who allegedly said it had, throughout much of his career, a really amazing afro. In a moment, we'll see if anybody can guess his name.

32

Being a Professional

Prof. Barry: Here are some key details. The person with the really amazing afro first started impressing people in the 1960s in pick-up basketball games in Harlem's Rucker Park. He then moved on to the University of Massachusetts and the ABA before eventually winning an NBA championship with the Philadelphia 76ers.

Ms. Bristol: I think I might know.

Prof. Barry: Good. We'll see if these next tidbits clinch it for you.

Ms. Bristol: Okay.

Prof. Barry: As stylish as he was dominant, this player had his jersey retired not just by the 76ers but also by the New Jersey Nets. Not too many players get even one team to honor them in that way, let alone two. He was even named one of *GQ*'s 25 Coolest Athletes of All Time in 2011, along with folks like Joe Namath and Muhammad Ali. No doubt his afro—and his rockin' white Converse All Stars—played some role in that. Want to tell everybody his name, Ms. Bristol?

Ms. Bristol: Julius Erving.

Prof. Barry: Better known as?

Ms. Bristol: Dr. J.

Prof. Barry: That's right: Dr. J. Would you now please read something Dr. J supposedly once told the Pulitzer Prize–winning journalist David Halberstam? Or maybe it was something Halberstam just knew Dr. J said at some point. Either way, it's pretty good.

Ms. Bristol: "Being a professional is doing the things you love to do, on the days you don't feel like doing them."

Prof. Barry: Here's how I think that sentiment applies to this class. If you are anything like previous students who have taken it, you will all soon begin to enjoy, even love, writing—but there will be days when you won't want to type a word. You'll be tired. You'll be worried about an exam. You'll be moping about a breakup. You'll be, I have no illusions, hungover.

I want you to nevertheless commit to make a Dr. J–esque pledge to doing something important as a condition of staying enrolled in this class.

Ms. Bristol: What?

Prof. Barry: Write. Every. Day.

Ms. Bristol: Even on weekends?

Prof. Barry: Even on weekends.

Ms. Bristol: Including football weekends?

Prof. Barry: Including football weekends. Sneak it in during halftime.

Ms. Bristol: That's a lot of writing.

Prof. Barry: Yes. It is. And a bunch of it will be bad—really, really bad. But that's okay. Later in the semester, we'll talk about what the writer Anne Lamott calls "Shitty First Drafts" and the importance writing expert Peter Elbow places on giving yourself a chance to unload, through unjudged ramblings, the "garbage in your head."

In fact, I want to give you all a little taste of Elbow's ideas right now. The quicker everybody in here abandons perfectionism and embraces Elbow's suggestion that "a person's best writing is often all mixed up with their worst," the quicker we can break the paralysis that sometimes comes from staring at a blank page. So here, Ms. Bristol, is an excerpt from Elbow's 1973 book *Writing without Teachers*. Read it for us, please.

Ms. Bristol: "There is garbage in your head; if you don't let it out onto paper, it really will infect everything else up there. Garbage in your head poisons you. Garbage on paper can safely be put in the wastepaper basket."

Prof. Barry: Or how about this next section. Elbow is describing the obstacles people sometimes create for themselves when they don't separate the drafting process from the editing process and instead immediately—and cripplingly—judge their sentences the moment they generate them.

Ms. Bristol: "It's an unnecessary burden to try to think of words and also worry at the same time whether they're the right words."

Prof. Barry: And finally, still from *Writing without Teachers*, here's a potentially helpful metaphor for the kind of patience and persistence we are going to need as writers.

Ms. Bristol: "Producing writing is not so much like filling a basin or pool once, but rather getting water to keep flowing through till finally it runs clear."

Prof. Barry: Isn't that a great image? All that muddy water coming out before you get something worth using.

Ms. Bristol: Yeah. It's like you have to turn yourself into a Brita filter.

Prof. Barry: Exactly. Editing is kind of like becoming a Brita filter. You start out with a mix of good and bad stuff, not really knowing the difference. And then slowly, sometimes *very* slowly, the good stuff eventually makes its way through, and the bad stuff gets left behind.

Ms. Bristol: Right.

Prof. Barry: We'll talk more about editing as the semester goes on. But what I want to do now is tell you all another story.

Ms. Bristol: About what?

Prof. Barry: About me.

Ms. Bristol: Yeah?

Prof. Barry: Yeah. It's from when I was living in Scotland, after college, in a city called Aberdeen. For a little while, I had a stalker. Or at least I thought I did.

33

All Football Comes from Stagg

Ms. Ida: You lived in Scotland?

Prof. Barry: I did.

Ms. Ida: For how long?

Prof. Barry: About a year.

Ms. Ida: Doing what?

Prof. Barry: Playing soccer.

Ms. Ida: Professionally?

Prof. Barry: Kind of.

Ms. Ida: You were a professional soccer player? In Scotland?

Prof. Barry: And back here in the US for a little while for a team called the Rochester Rhinos. But "professional soccer player" is a bit generous. I was more like a professional practice player.

Ms. Ida: You rode the bench?

Prof. Barry: Big time. I was definitely the worst one on the team.

Ms. Ida: That sucks.

Prof. Barry: Not really. I never intended soccer to be my career. Particularly when I was in Scotland, it was more like an extended study abroad trip. The added bonus was that I got to wear shin guards to work.

Mr. Dewey (*jumping in*): This was after you graduated college?

Prof. Barry: Yeah.

Mr. Dewey (*incredulously*): From the University of Chicago?

Prof. Barry: I know. Chicago is not exactly known for being an athletic powerhouse. A past president, Robert Maynard Hutchins, is said to have lived by a motto that goes something like this: "Anytime I feel like exercising, I lie down until that feeling goes away." The phrasing of the motto varies and has been credited to a whole bunch of people other than Hutchins, including Mark Twain. But it definitely reflects the shift away from athletics that Hutchins's administration brought about at Chicago. Before he arrived, the school was actually a big force in the world of college athletics. Where do you think the phrase "Monsters of the Midway" comes from?

Mr. Dewey: I thought it started with the Chicago Bears?

Prof. Barry: Nope. It started with the University of Chicago football team. The coach was a guy named Amos Alonzo Stagg. He was a real pioneer when it came to things like using a huddle, sending a player in motion, and, I think, having players wear uniforms with numbers on them.

Mr. Dewey: Uniforms didn't used to have numbers on them?

Prof. Barry: Not before Stagg. He created a lot of things we now take for granted. It's sort of like a famous compliment paid by Ernest Hemingway to Mark Twain. "All American literature,"

Hemingway wrote in 1935, "comes from one book by Mark Twain called *Huckleberry Finn*."

Mr. Dewey: So what—all football comes from Amos Alonzo Stagg?

Prof. Barry: Kind of. Or at least that's what Knute Rockne, the legendary football coach at Notre Dame, once said.

Mr. Dewey: Really?

Prof. Barry: Yeah. He said, "All football comes from Stagg."

Mr. Dewey: That's pretty cool.

Prof. Barry: What's even more impressive is that it's not just football that comes from Stagg. One of the players Stagg coached during his career eventually made quite a difference in another sport: basketball.

Any guesses who it might be?

Ms. Bristol (*jumping in*): Are you going to say Coach K again? Because I am not sure I'll believe you.

Prof. Barry: No. I'm not going to say Coach K again. I'm going to say Coach N, as in Coach James Naismith. Or maybe you have heard him referred to as Dr. James Naismith.

Ms. Bristol: You mean the guy who invented basketball?

Prof. Barry: Yeah. Do you know where Naismith did that? Do you know where he put up his famous first peach basket and had people try to get a ball to land inside it?

Ms. Bristol: Springfield, Massachusetts?

Prof. Barry: Yup. At what is now called Springfield College. So take a guess where Stagg's first coaching gig was?

Ms. Bristol: Seriously? It was at Springfield College?

Prof. Barry: Seriously. Naismith played on the football team Stagg formed there in 1890, a year before Naismith and his peach baskets made history in the school's gym. Stagg even played in the first public basketball game, scoring the only basket for the faculty side in a 5–1 loss to the students.

He also, after bringing basketball to the University of Chicago, helped change the game from nine players versus nine players—which is how Naismith originally organized the sport—to the modern five-on-five format.

All this helps explain why, in addition to being in the College Football Hall of Fame, Stagg is also in the Basketball Hall of Fame, right there with his Canadian friend.

Ms. Bristol: Canadian friend?

Prof. Barry: Yeah, James Naismith. Naismith is Canadian. He was born in Ontario.

Ms. Bristol: The guy who invented basketball is Canadian?

Prof. Barry: Surprising, right? Sort of like how the guy who created hockey's Stanley Cup was actually British.

Ms. Bristol: Really?

Prof. Barry: Yeah. His name is Lord Frederick Arthur Stanley. He was the sixteenth Earl of Derby, and he didn't grow up in a hockey-mad town like Toronto, Montreal, or Vancouver. Instead, he grew up in London. I'm not sure he even knew how to skate.

34
Pack a Pillow

Prof. Barry: You can still see the legacy of Amos Alonzo Stagg if you go to the University of Chicago. I played soccer, for example, on Stagg Field, and during my senior year, I actually won something called the Stagg Medal. But let's be clear: Stagg was much better at both football and basketball than I was at soccer. By the time I enrolled, Chicago was far removed from its time as a Division 1 school. It's not like I was David Beckham or anything.

My experience playing in Scotland was instead more like a kind of postcollege study abroad trip, something I did because I was young, relatively unencumbered, and very, very fortunate to have people tell me that the chance to explore another country—particularly a country as wonderful and welcoming as Scotland—should not be ignored. In some ways, it is as if I followed the advice Jhumpa Lahiri offers in her novel *The Namesake*. Want to read that advice for us, Ms. Henrietta?

Ms. Henrietta: "You are still young. Free."

Prof. Barry: Keep going.

Ms. Henrietta: "Do yourself a favor. Before it's too late, without thinking too much about it first, pack a pillow and a blanket and see as much of the world as you can. You will not regret it. One day it will be too late."

Prof. Barry: So that's kind of what I did. Only instead of packing a pillow, I packed my soccer ball.

Ms. Ida (*jumping in*): Who packed the stalker?

Prof. Barry: We are about to find out.

35
Bunk Bed

Prof. Barry: To set the scene a bit, I was twenty-three years old when I went to Scotland. I didn't have any family there. I didn't have any friends. I didn't even speak the language.

Mr. Leigh: Don't they speak English in Scotland?

Prof. Barry: Technically, yes. But linguistically, the English that people speak in Scotland is a lot different than, say, the English that people speak in Ireland, or the English that people speak in Wales, or even the English that people speak in England.

And all of those are even more different than the English that people speak in the United States. As the Irish playwright George Bernard Shaw supposedly once quipped, "The United States and Great Britain are two countries separated by a common language."

Mr. Leigh: I think I've heard that before.

Prof. Barry: There's a similar line in a short story by Oscar Wilde, "The Canterville Ghost." A character says at one point, "We have really everything in common with America nowadays, except, of course, our ______." Any guess what goes in that blank?

Mr. Leigh: The word *language*?

Prof. Barry: Right. The character says, "We have really everything in common with America nowadays, except, of course, our language."

And to give you some sense of how big the linguistic difference is, I'll share that when one of my sisters came to visit me in Scotland, she had such a hard time understanding the words she heard on the street that she essentially asked me to be her translator.

Ms. Yona (*jumping in*): My roommate is Scottish.

Prof. Barry: Yeah?

Ms. Yona: Yeah. She grew up in Edinburgh.

Prof. Barry: Do you notice any language differences, even in just the names you each have for different things?

Ms. Yona: Sometimes, yeah.

Prof. Barry: Does she call an elevator a "lift"?

Ms. Yona: Yup.

Prof. Barry: And potato chips a bag of "crisps"?

Ms. Yona: Yeah, that one really confused me at first.

Prof. Barry: How about "torch" for flashlight and "hoover" for vacuum?

Ms. Yona: Definitely. And she's also got this amazing word to describe when two people are messily making out, like on a bar's dance floor or something. She calls it "snogging." I love that.

Prof. Barry: "Snogging" was definitely one of my favorite words over there. I know it can be used to describe an ordinary kiss. But to me, it just sounds so hilariously sloppy and public and drunken. I can hear the slobbery, wet noise of a snog every time someone says the word. It's almost like an onomatopoeia.

Ms. Yona: The thing I always think about with "snogging" is a celebrity getting caught with a nanny.

Prof. Barry: I could see that.

Ms. Yona: Were there any of those types of scandals while you were in Scotland?

Prof. Barry: Probably. But to be honest, I was relatively cut off from the world, especially in the beginning. I didn't know anybody. I didn't know where anything was.

Ms. Yona: Where were you living?

Prof. Barry: In a dorm.

Ms. Yona: In a dorm? You were living in a dorm? Like a college dorm? With students?

Prof. Barry: Yeah, I know. It was kind of embarrassing. Here I was, trying to be a professional soccer player: I had my cleats, or what the Scottish call "boots"; I had my uniform, or what the Scottish call "a kit"; and yet every night, I would go home, depressingly, to a bunk bed. Fortunately, the experience didn't last very long. When some of my teammates found out about my situation, they tried to help me out. There was only one problem.

Ms. Yona: What?

Prof. Barry: Their help is actually how I ended up with a stalker.

36

Perspective-Taking

Prof. Barry: The teammate who helped me out the most was the right fullback, a young guy named Andy. Super nice. Super talented. I think at the time he was playing for one of Scotland's Youth National Teams. Maybe the Under-20s. Maybe the Under-19s. I can't remember exactly. All I know is that he had a friend who knew somebody who owned a bed-and-breakfast.

Ms. Yona: You moved from a dorm to a bed-and-breakfast? Couldn't you find anything more permanent?

Prof. Barry: You don't understand. Andy said this bed-and-breakfast was *incredible,* particularly because of the woman who ran it: Barbara.

Ms. Yona: Barbara?

Prof. Barry: Yeah. Barbara. I was told she was a great cook. I was told she was a great host. And I was also told that for the right lodger—one who was responsible, and was quiet, and didn't cause any problems—she would even consider renting out one of the place's rooms on a more long-term basis. It seemed like a really good deal.

Ms. Yona: Was the house nice?

Prof. Barry: Very. Stone architecture. Pristine lawn. Wonderful location. Close enough to the main streets of Aberdeen for me to walk to everything I needed, but also far enough away from them so I didn't have to contend, at all hours of the night, with the interrupting sounds of traffic.

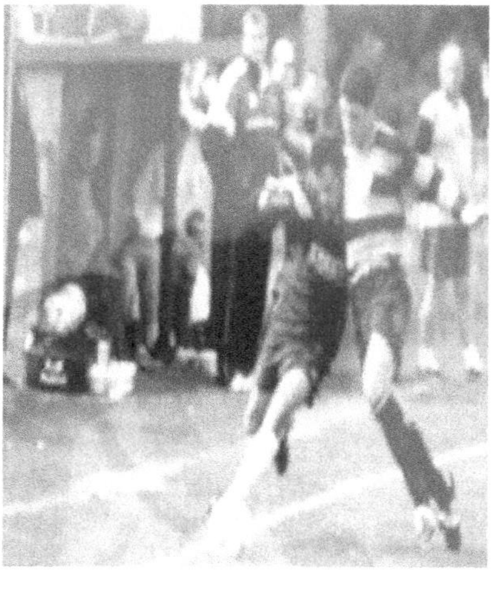

Ms. Yona: That seems like a good setup.

Prof. Barry: Doesn't it? And Barbara herself was extremely warm and friendly when she opened the door.

But then I turned to my left and saw the following picture on the wall, in a frame, sort of centered and made the focus of the hallway. The image is, I'm sorry, a little blurry, but with any luck you can still identify me on the right side of it.

Ms. Yona: That's you in the striped shirt?

Prof. Barry: Yup.

Ms. Yona: And it was hanging in Barbara's hallway?

Prof. Barry: Yeah, in a frame.

Ms. Yona: But you had never met her before?

Prof. Barry: Right.

Ms. Yona: You had never talked on the phone?

Prof. Barry: Nope.

Ms. Nina (*jumping in*): Exchanged emails?

Prof. Barry: Nope.

Ms. Nina: Did you send her a text with this photo, so she'd recognize you when you arrived?

Prof. Barry: I didn't even know the photo existed.

Ms. Nina: Then where did she get it?

Prof. Barry: The newspaper.

Ms. Nina: She got the photo from the *newspaper*?

Prof. Barry: Yup.

Ms. Nina: Weird.

Prof. Barry: More than weird. Frightening.

Ms. Henrietta (*jumping in*): I would have freaked out if I saw a picture of me in a stranger's house, especially if it was taken from a newspaper. That's really creepy.

Prof. Barry: I did freak out. I did find it creepy. I almost turned around and ran out the door.

Ms. Henrietta: Why didn't you?

Prof. Barry: Because I noticed that Barbara was as startled as I was.

Ms. Henrietta: What do you mean?

Prof. Barry: I mean that as I was turning to leave, I saw her look at the picture, look at me, look back at the picture, and then kind of shutter.

Ms. Henrietta: Like she had been caught stalking you?

Prof. Barry: No. It wasn't the shutter of a stalker—it was the shutter of somebody who suddenly thought *she* had a stalker.

Ms. Henrietta: Really?

Prof. Barry: Yeah. Any idea why? I'll actually open this question up to the entire class: Can anyone explain why, when Barbara and I each looked at that picture of me hanging on her wall, I thought she was stalking me and she thought I was stalking her?

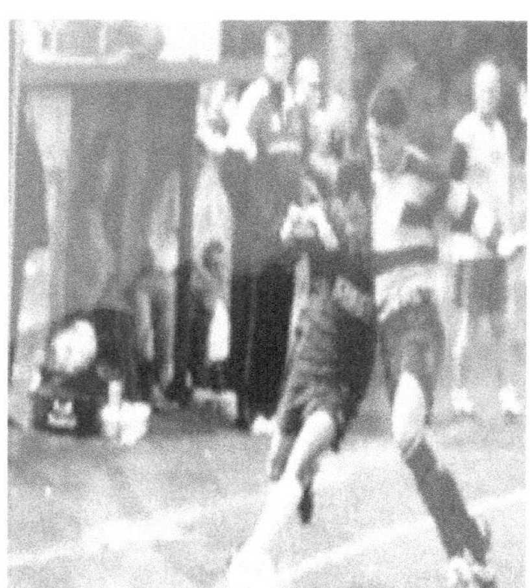

You may want to take another look at the picture and ask the following question: Who is the picture actually of?

Think about audience. Think about our earlier examples from the 2013 Ouch-Back Bowl and the 2012 Ryder Cup and how the same event can seem like a bitter defeat to one set of people but like a thrilling victory to another set of people. Looked at in a certain way, by a certain person, that picture may not be of me at all.

37

Scottie

Ms. Henrietta: Are you saying that's not you in the picture, wearing the striped shirt?

Prof. Barry: That's definitely me in the picture, wearing the striped shirt. The question is: Even though it's me, is that really a picture *of* me, at least in the eyes of everyone who might view it?

Ms. Ida (*jumping in*): Like Barbara?

Prof. Barry: Yeah. Like Barbara. Think about who else might be, to Barbara, the focus of the picture. The answer could help you understand why she reacted the way she did.

Ms. Ida: Did she know one of the other people in the photo?

Prof. Barry: Good.

Ms. Ida: Did she know the player you're competing against?

Prof. Barry: She did. Turns out that's Scottie.

Ms. Ida: Who's Scottie?

Prof. Barry: Her son.

Ms. Ida: I see. So that's not really a picture of you, at least in Barbara's eyes. It's a picture of Scottie.

Prof. Barry: Right.

Ms. Ida: You're just some random guy trying to steal the ball from her son.

Prof. Barry: Until?

Ms. Ida: Until you showed up at her door.

Prof. Barry: Then what did I become?

Ms. Ida: An unsettling coincidence.

Prof. Barry: The kind of unsettling coincidence that could make someone think, *Um, is this guy a stalker?*

Ms. Ida: Maybe. Yeah.

Prof. Barry: What do you think, Ms. Cawlow? We haven't heard from you yet today. Perhaps as an art history major—that's what you're studying here, right?

Ms. Cawlow: Right.

Prof. Barry: Well, perhaps that training means you can help us decode this picture. Would you have reacted the way I did when seeing it?

Ms. Cawlow: I think so. My first thought would probably have been *stalker* if what happened to you happened to me.

Prof. Barry: How about if what happened to Barbara happened to you?

Ms. Cawlow: You mean some random guy from a photo I owned showing up at my door?

Prof. Barry: Yeah. Would you have reacted the way she did? Would you have thought I was the stalker?

Ms. Cawlow: Probably. Random people in the background of pictures I own should stay random people in the background of pictures I own. They shouldn't knock on my door.

Prof. Barry: Good. The background status of me in that picture is precisely the point. Not every picture of me is a picture of me, at least not to everyone who looks at it. The same is true of pictures of all of you. Our self-absorption may lead us to believe that we are the star of every photo, the focus of every group shot. But the truth is probably closer to a bit of wisdom attributed to President Franklin Roosevelt. Can you please read it for us?

Ms. Cawlow: "Remember you are just an extra in everyone else's play."

Prof. Barry: It wasn't until my encounter with Barbara, twenty-three years into my life, that I started to understand the wisdom of FDR's advice.

But perhaps you've all had a similar experience. Think of a time when you've shown some friends what you consider a really great picture of a bunch of you. In your mind, the picture captures the incredible warmth and joy and kindness you bring out in each other. But then one of your friends objects. "That's a terrible picture," they say. "I look fat."

Ms. Ida (*jumping in*)**:** My mom does that all the time. I think her definition of a family photo is a photo where she looks great and the rest of us happen to be nearby.

Prof. Barry: In *Rosencrantz and Guildenstern Are Dead*, the playwright Tom Stoppard has a lot of fun with this kind of perspective-taking. He moves Hamlet, perhaps the most famous character in Western literature, to the periphery and instead retells Shakespeare's story from the viewpoint of two very minor characters: Rosencrantz and Guildenstern. He also includes the following wonderful line. Read it for us please, Ms. Cawlow.

Ms. Cawlow: "Look on every exit as an entrance somewhere else."

Prof. Barry: What's going on there? How might Stoppard's phrasing fit into what we have been discussing today? In what way is it an example of word choice shifting our perspective and changing the world people see?

Ms. Cawlow: Maybe because it's like the optimistic advice, "When one door closes, another door opens"?

Prof. Barry: Maybe. But I'm not sure Tom Stoppard was being that sanguine. There is an acerbic, even morbid wit running through a lot of the play. Plus, I mostly like the line for its more literal point. For example, if you, Ms. Cawlow, got up and walked through that door over there, we could say that you exited the classroom, right?

Ms. Cawlow: Right.

Prof. Barry: But we could also say?

Ms. Cawlow: I entered the hall.

Prof. Barry: Exactly. Just like when National Book Award winner Colson Whitehead writes in his novel *Sag Harbor* that "her breast grazed my elbow," it is no surprise that he then writes this next sentence.

Ms. Cawlow: "Or my elbow grazed her breast, depending on your perspective."

Prof. Barry: And how about the following passage from *Flaubert's Parrot*, a novel by another award-winning writer, Julian Barnes?

Ms. Cawlow: "You can define a net in one of two ways, depending on your point of view. Normally you would say that it is a meshed instrument designed to catch fish. But you could, with no great injury to logic, reverse the image and define a net as a jocular lexicographer once did: he called it a collection of holes tied together with string."

Prof. Barry: "A collection of holes tied together with string"—isn't that a brilliant way to describe a net?

Ms. Cawlow: Yeah. It's like those pictures that are optical illusions—the ones where, at first, you think you are looking at an old woman and then, a second later, the image changes into a young woman.

Prof. Barry: Exactly. Only here the shift in focus occurs entirely through language. Which, as I said, is a nice reminder of today's key principle. What is it again?

Ms. Cawlow: The words you choose can change the world people see.

Prof. Barry: Good—though as we are about to see, there is a bit more to it than that.

38

Joseph M. Williams

Prof. Barry: To explain what I mean, I want to introduce you to the work of Joseph Williams, who taught writing for many years at the University of Chicago.

Ms. Cawlow: Did he teach you?

Prof. Barry: No. But many of the people he taught eventually taught me. And they were great. They're the ones who first showed me the trick I want to now show all of you: how to refocus sentences.

Ms. Cawlow: Got it.

Prof. Barry: Let's start with a sentence from *Style: Toward Clarity and Grace*, a wonderful book Williams wrote with Greg Colomb back in 1990. Would you mind reading it for us, please, Mr. Marshall? You might like the content, given all the prelaw stuff on your résumé.

Mr. Marshall: Is the sentence about law?

Prof. Barry: Yeah. It is taken from what seems to be a legal brief in a medical malpractice case. Here it is.

Mr. Marshall: "A patient whose reactions go unmonitored may also claim physician liability."

Prof. Barry: What I want you to do is read the follow-up sentences and then see how Williams refocuses each of them to better make the patient's case. I think it will teach us a lot about "the infinite power of grammar," a phrase we'll return to later with the help of the great writer Joan Didion.

Mr. Marshall: Okay.

Prof. Barry: So start from the top.

Mr. Marshall: With the sentence I just read?

Prof. Barry: Yeah. With the sentence you just read. I've underlined the part that we are going to refocus.

Mr. Marshall: "A patient whose reactions go unmonitored may also claim physician liability."

Prof. Barry: Now read the next sentence.

Mr. Marshall: "In this case, a patient took Cloromax as prescribed, which resulted in partial renal failure."

Prof. Barry: And the next one.

Mr. Marshall: "The manufacturer's literature indicated that the patient should be observed frequently and should immediately report any sign of infection."

Prof. Barry: And now read the final two, together.

Mr. Marshall: "Evidence indicated that the patient had not received instructions to report any signs of urinary blockage. Moreover, the patient had no white cell count taken until after he developed the blockage."

Prof. Barry: Good. Any guesses why I underlined "patient" in all those sentences?

Mr. Marshall: To show that the focus is always on the same subject?

Prof. Barry: Partly. But also to show that the focus is perhaps on the *wrong* subject, at least if you are trying to build a case for medical malpractice.

Mr. Marshall: I'm not sure I follow.

Prof. Barry: Think of it this way: What's the potential problem with making the patient the focus of all those sentences, with linking his actions to the renal failure he eventually suffered?

Mr. Marshall: It makes him seem responsible for the renal failure. It makes the patient seem like the wrongdoer.

Prof. Barry: Exactly. The students I teach over at the law school often make a similar mistake. They come into the Human Trafficking Clinic or they come into the Child Welfare Appellate Clinic, and without really thinking, they immediately focus their sentences on the client's actions.

Why do you think that is? Why is immediately focusing sentences on the client's actions actually a pretty understandable, even admirable error to commit if you are a law student?

Mr. Marshall: Because it's probably good to relate to and empathize with the clients you represent.

Prof. Barry: And make sure their story gets heard, right?

Mr. Marshall: Right.

Prof. Barry: Do you think it's fair to assume that my students take seriously their responsibility to tell those stories, to advocate on behalf of their clients?

Mr. Marshall: I would hope so.

Prof. Barry: So their initial impulse might be to do what, do you think?

Mr. Marshall: Frame the story from their client's point of view.

Prof. Barry: Even though?

Mr. Marshall: Even though that might not be the best strategy in every case.

Prof. Barry: Just like it might not be the best strategy in every ad campaign, or product pitch, or public policy initiative. Later in class, for example, we are going to see how a clever change in focus helped Adam Grant, a psychologist at the Wharton School of Business, get doctors to wash their hands more. With a little bit of imagination—and reorientation—he provided a way to reduce the spread of disease.

But first we are going to do some nitty-gritty work with the sentences you just read, Mr. Marshall. I want to make sure that when all of you are presented with an opportunity to refocus a sentence, you know the editing options available to you.

39

Malpractice or Mal-patient

Prof. Barry: Please read that first sentence one more time, Mr. Marshall. Then we'll read the same sentence rewritten by Joe Williams.

Mr. Marshall: "A patient whose reactions go unmonitored may also claim physician liability."

Prof. Barry: Now as rewritten by Williams.

Mr. Marshall: "If a physician does not monitor his patient's reactions, he may be held liable."

Prof. Barry: Notice the difference?

Mr. Marshall: Yeah.

Prof. Barry: What is it?

Mr. Marshall: In the second one, where the physician is the focus, the lack of monitoring seems more clearly his fault, not the patient's.

Prof. Barry: That becomes even more evident in the next edit. Read the original for us.

Mr. Marshall: "In this case, a patient took Cloromax as prescribed, which resulted in partial renal failure."

Prof. Barry: And now the rewrite.

Mr. Marshall: "In this case, the physician prescribed Cloromax, *which caused the patient to experience partial renal failure.*"

Prof. Barry: You see what that shift in focus opens up?

Mr. Marshall: Yeah. The chance to link something the physician did to the pain the patient experienced.

Prof. Barry: Exactly. That's why I put the second part in italics. I wanted to highlight how, because of the edit, the sentence now establishes a much more damning cause-and-effect relationship. The same is true of the next two sentences. Start with the original again, please.

Mr. Marshall: "The manufacturer's literature indicated that the patient should be observed frequently and should immediately report any sign of infection. Evidence indicated that the patient had not received instructions to report any signs of urinary blockage."

Prof. Barry: And now the Joe Williams version.

Mr. Marshall: "The physician had been cautioned by the manufacturer's literature that he should observe the patient frequently and instruct the patient to report any sign of infection. Evidence indicates that the physician also failed to instruct the patient to report any sign of urinary blockage."

Prof. Barry: Notice the ingenuity required to refocus that sentence. Williams takes a document that could be seen as a resource for the patient and reframes it as, essentially, a warning to the physician. "The physician had been cautioned by the manufacturer's literature." That's pretty creative and sly. And what a great, great verb "cautioned" is, right?

Why do you think I say that, Mr. Marshall? What makes "cautioned" such a great choice for that sentence? What work is it doing?

Mr. Marshall: It creates the sense that the physician was reckless, or at least negligent. Like he ignored a clear instruction.

Prof. Barry: And how about the choice of "also" in "Evidence indicates that the physician also failed to instruct"? What effect does adding that word have?

Mr. Marshall: It signals that the physician made a bunch of errors, that his mistakes are really piling up.

Prof. Barry: Good. Verlyn Klinkenborg, a longtime member of the editorial team at the *New York Times*, has a neat way of describing this kind of linking, one sentence acknowledging and building off the ones that came before it. In a book called *Several Short Sentences on Writing*, he celebrates the way writers like Jane Austen make sure that successive sentences "listen to one another."

Isn't that great? I love the idea that Austen's sentences are listening to one another, as if they each have these wonderfully big, attentive, almost Dumbo-like ears.

Mr. Marshall: Yeah.

Prof. Barry: And perhaps that is what's going on with the *also* in Williams's rewrite. It shows that the sentence helpfully listened to the one before it and is now including a supporting point.

Mr. Marshall: Right.

Prof. Barry: We'll talk more about how to do that later in the semester, when we return to Williams's book and look at something he calls moving from "old information to new information."

But before going any farther, I want to ask something about the material we just covered: Did it make anybody uncomfortable that, just by switching the focus of those sentences in the malpractice case, we could essentially shift the blame from the patient to the doctor? Did anyone get nervous about what the power and flexibility of language can do?

40

Nobody Has a Monopoly on Effective Language

Prof. Barry: Here's a follow-up question to the one I just posed: While Mr. Marshall and I were rearranging the relationship between the patient and the doctor, did anyone think, "You know, I'm not sure I like that something so consequential can be reframed, even manipulated, so easily?"

Mr. Carlos: I guess I did, at least a little.

Prof. Barry: And you are?

Mr. Carlos: Mr. Carlos.

Prof. Barry: Right. You're one of the premed students, right?

Mr. Carlos: Yeah.

Prof. Barry: That makes sense then. I could see why you might get a little uncomfortable with the reframing. Once you become a doctor, you're not going to want a malpractice suit to turn on a bit of compositional creativity, are you?

Mr. Carlos: No.

Prof. Barry: This might sound a bit disingenuous given that I teach at the law school, but I feel the same way. The manipulation of words and sentences often makes me a bit uneasy—especially when I remember that nobody has a monopoly on effective language. Many glorious deeds have been helped along by effective language, but many terrible deeds have as well.

Mr. Carlos: That's what I was thinking. I would want to know who actually messed up—the doctor or the patient—before signing on to one of those sentences.

Prof. Barry: Or think of something much more grave and terrible, like the rhetorical manipulation that often accompanies, or even leads to, mass murder. The Rwandan Genocide, the Armenian Genocide, the Khmer Rouge in Cambodia—all of these horrors were fueled by insidiously effective language. During the Rwandan Genocide, for example, hundreds of thousands of innocent Tutsi people were labeled "cockroaches" and other dehumanizing names by their rivals, the Hutus. What do you think that did to how people viewed Tutsis? What does the term *cockroach* imply?

Mr. Carlos: That they should be exterminated.

Prof. Barry: Exactly. Or think of the Nazis.

Mr. Carlos: Yeah. Wasn't Hitler known for being really good with language?

Prof. Barry: He was. But the sample bit of propaganda I want us to look at actually comes from Heinrich Himmler, who built and oversaw many of the Nazi concentration camps. Himmler also ran the Gestapo, which is the name of the secret police force that terrorized citizens for more than a decade. Read the following lines for us, please, Mr. Carlos. It contains an unfortunately common tactic in genocidal rhetoric: using the term *lice* to refer to people you despise.

Mr. Carlos: "Antisemitism is exactly the same as delousing. Getting rid of lice is not a question of ideology. It is a matter of cleanliness."

Prof. Barry: Keep going.

Mr. Carlos: "In just the same way, antisemitism, for us, has not been a question of ideology, but a matter of cleanliness, which now will soon have been dealt with. We shall soon be deloused. We have only 20,000 lice left, and then the matter is finished within the whole of Germany."

Prof. Barry: Starting to see where the term *ethnic cleansing* comes from?

Mr. Carlos: Unfortunately.

41

Michael King Day

Prof. Barry: It can be pretty dispiriting to read accounts like Himmler's. Or certainly whole books on genocide, like Philip Gourevitch's *We Wish to Inform You That Tomorrow We Will Be Killed along with Our Families,* which looks at the genocide in Rwanda; Peter Balakian's *Black Dog of Fate,* which looks at the genocide in Armenia; or Samantha Powers's *A Problem from Hell,* which looks at several genocides at once. Each of these books, by the way, I highly recommend.

Mr. Carlos: You recommend books that are dispiriting?

Prof. Barry: The subject matter can be dispiriting. But the books themselves are, I think, uplifting. None tries to ignore the brutal horror and devastation in the events it covers. None treats the victims as too remote to care about or the perpetrators as too monstrous to understand. None gives in to apathy, cynicism, or indifference. Instead, all make heroic efforts to grapple with some of the worst atrocities in human history, to bear witness, to tell an important story, to document and correct wrongs that many would prefer not to think about and some have even worked vigorously to cover up.

And here's the really uplifting part: all of them do this using tools entirely at our disposal. They use words. They use sentences. They

use paragraphs. "If you want to change the world," these books show, "pick up your pen and write."

Ms. Toth (*jumping in*): I think I've seen that on a T-shirt somewhere.

Prof. Barry: I have too, usually attributed to Martin Luther—the sixteenth-century German theologian, not the twentieth-century civil rights icon. Have you ever heard of him?

Ms. Toth: Is he the guy with the "95 Theses"?

Prof. Barry: Yeah, that's him. His written words have had an enormous influence on the world. He helped shape the Protestant Reformation, and he is also a big reason we celebrate something called Martin Luther King Day.

Ms. Toth: I thought you said Martin Luther and Martin Luther King are two different people.

Prof. Barry: They are. But there wouldn't have been a Martin Luther King Jr. without Martin Luther—or at least not one by that specific name. Anybody know why?

Mr. Marshall (*jumping in*): I do.

Prof. Barry: Yeah?

Mr. Marshall: Yeah. Martin Luther King Jr. wasn't born "Martin Luther King Jr."

Prof. Barry: What was he born?

Mr. Marshall: He was born Michael King Jr.

Prof. Barry: Because?

Mr. Marshall: He was named after his father, Michael King Sr., who was also a minister.

Prof. Barry: But then?

Mr. Marshall: But then, when Michael King Jr.—the eventual civil rights leader—was five years old, Michael King Sr. visited a bunch of holy sites in Germany.

Prof. Barry: What happened during the trip?

Mr. Marshall: His father became very inspired by the life of theologian Martin Luther.

Prof. Barry: And then what?

Mr. Marshall: He decided to change his own name to Martin Luther.

Prof. Barry: But he kept his last name.

Mr. Marshall: Right.

Prof. Barry: So his full name became?

Mr. Marshall: Martin Luther King.

Prof. Barry: Which meant his son's name became?

Mr. Marshall: Martin Luther King Jr.

Prof. Barry: Which is why, every January, we celebrate not "Michael King Day" but "Martin Luther King Day."

42

Trying Is Cool

Prof. Barry: I want to return to that quote you said you once saw on a T-shirt, Ms. Toth.

Ms. Toth: "If you want to change the world, pick up your pen and write"?

Prof. Barry: Yeah. I wonder if we might be able to rephrase it a bit and create our own version. You up for that?

Ms. Toth: Sure. Rumor has it, "Trying is cool."

Prof. Barry: That's right. Trying is cool. Very cool. Did you get that from one of my former students?

Ms. Toth: Yeah. My roommate took this course last year. And your other course.

Prof. Barry: The Syntax of Slavery?

Ms. Toth: Yup.

Prof. Barry: And so she told you about "Trying is cool"?

Ms. Toth: For a while, it was written on our refrigerator.

Prof. Barry: With what?

Ms. Toth: You know those magnets that have random words on them? They're black and white—or at least ours were—and you can arrange them in like a million different combinations.

Prof. Barry: Yeah, I know those.

Ms. Toth: One of the combinations, for about two months, was "Trying is cool."

Prof. Barry: Nice.

Ms. Toth: She said it's a theme of your classes.

Prof. Barry: That's right. It is a theme, a very important theme. Too many students approach school with a fear of failure—with some warped notion that if they try something and mess up, they are going to reveal some fundamental flaw in their intelligence and character. It's a real handicap, as psychologists like Stanford's Carol Dweck have shown.

So what we'll try to do this semester is put a premium on effort and experimentation, on developing new skills and embracing difficult challenges. The line "Trying is cool" is one motto for that, but others certainly exist. Take these next lines from *The Cantos*, an epic poem by the modernist writer Ezra Pound. Can you read them for us, Ms. Toth?

Ms. Toth:

> *Here error is all in the not done,*
> *all in the diffidence that faltered*

Prof. Barry: Pound not only produced his own works in the early twentieth century; he also helped a lot of other great writers produce theirs, including Ernest Hemingway, Marianne Moore, and T. S. Eliot. In fact, I sometimes teach law students about editing by pointing out some of the help Pound gave Eliot on Eliot's most famous poem, *The Waste Land*.

But for now, we can at least use Pound's lines from *The Cantos* to adopt a mindset worth immediately implementing. In this course, error will be "all in the not done," in paragraphs not attempted, in ideas not explored, in chances not taken. So don't be shy about trying new approaches and techniques. Don't, in other words, let your diffidence falter.

Or if you prefer a sportier message, here's a great sentence from *The Art of Fielding*, a novel that centers around a supremely gifted college shortstop named Henry. The sentence describes what motivates him when he's playing his beloved position.

Ms. Toth: "To reach a ball he has never reached before, to extend himself to the very limits of his range, and then a step farther: this is the shortstop's dream."

Prof. Barry: We are not going to necessarily reach for groundballs in this class, but I will ask you to extend yourself to the very limits of your range—and then a step farther. I will ask you to grow, to develop, to become, in the words of Samuel Beckett's great fictional creation Molloy, at least "a little less, in the end, the creature you were in the beginning, and the middle."

I will also ask you to take seriously the power of words. Do you remember Tom Stoppard? We talked about his play *Rosencrantz and Guildenstern Are Dead* a little earlier in the class.

Ms. Toth: Yeah. He's the guy who wrote, "Look on every exit as an entrance somewhere else."

Prof. Barry: Right. The lead character in one of his other plays, *The Real Thing*, offers a pretty good argument for why we should treat words with reverence—why they deserve, as he says, respect.

Ms. Toth: "I don't think writers are sacred, but words are. They deserve respect. If you get the right ones in the right order, you might nudge the world a little."

Prof. Barry: Or how about this from James Baldwin, whose essays on racism and civil rights combined keen social observation with beautiful literary composition.

Ms. Toth: "You write in order to change the world, knowing perfectly well that you probably can't, but also knowing that literature is indispensable to the world. . . . The world changes according to the way people see it, and if you alter, even by a millimeter, the way a person looks or people look at reality, then you can change it."

Prof. Barry: Pretty good, huh?

Ms. Toth: Yeah.

Prof. Barry: You'll see that quote all over the internet, wherever writers can be found. But let's return to the world of sports for a moment, so we can look at a more concrete example of Baldwin's core message at work.

43

Buddy Ryan

Prof. Barry: Has anybody ever seen the ESPN documentary on the 1985 Chicago Bears?

Ms. Bristol (*jumping in*)**:** The *30 for 30* documentary?

Prof. Barry: Yeah, that one. Do you remember how it begins?

Ms. Bristol: With a letter.

Prof. Barry: Who writes the letter?

Ms. Bristol: The defensive players on the Bears.

Prof. Barry: Who receives the letter?

Ms. Bristol: George Halas.

Prof. Barry: Who's George Halas?

Ms. Bristol: At the time, he was the owner of the Bears.

Prof. Barry: So he's the audience of the letter? Remember that was one of our key terms from the beginning of class.

Ms. Bristol: Yeah.

Prof. Barry: And so then what's the function, our other key term? What is the letter trying *to do*?

Ms. Bristol: Persuade George Halas not to fire the defensive coordinator.

Prof. Barry: What's the role of a defensive coordinator?

Ms. Bristol: He is essentially the coach of the defense.

Prof. Barry: Why was the one on the Bears in danger of being fired?

Ms. Bristol: The Bears weren't doing well.

Prof. Barry: And?

Ms. Bristol: The players were afraid that Halas was going to fire the entire coaching staff.

Prof. Barry: What was the defensive coordinator's name, the one the players loved so much?

Ms. Bristol: Buddy Ryan.

Prof. Barry: And did their plan work? Did the letter they wrote persuade Halas not to fire Ryan?

Ms. Bristol: It did. Halas apparently said that he had never been prouder of his players than when he read that letter.

Prof. Barry: Then what happened?

Ms. Bristol: The defense Ryan designed became perhaps the most dominant defense in NFL history.

Prof. Barry: That's the defense that helped the Bears to a near-perfect season in 1985, including a record-breaking win in the Super Bowl, right?

Ms. Bristol: Right.

Prof. Barry: See, I told you: "If you want to change the world, pick up your pen and write." Without that letter, it's tough to imagine

the '85 Bears winning the Super Bowl or later getting invited to the White House by Barack Obama to celebrate the twenty-fifth anniversary of their victory.

Ms. Bristol: And that letter wasn't the only letter in the movie.

Prof. Barry: Oh, right. There's a letter at the end, isn't there? Who's the audience of that second letter?

Ms. Bristol: The defensive players who wrote the original letter.

Prof. Barry: What's the function?

Ms. Bristol: To thank them.

Prof. Barry: Who writes it?

Ms. Bristol: Buddy Ryan.

Prof. Barry: Back in 1985?

Ms. Bristol: No. A lot later, while Ryan was battling a third or fourth bout with cancer. All the players had long been retired.

Prof. Barry: What does he thank them for? Saving his job?

Ms. Bristol: That, and for giving him what he calls "the best memories of my coaching life." It's a really great letter. He addresses it "To My Guys."

Prof. Barry: Who reads it?

Ms. Bristol: The players do. Out loud.

Prof. Barry: All of them?

Ms. Bristol: No. Some of them are too touched to speak.

Prof. Barry: A few cry, don't they?

Ms. Bristol: Big time.

Prof. Barry: Think about that. A simple letter, a set of small scribbles and symbols on a single scrap of paper, can take some of the meanest, most aggressive, most hard-nosed football players ever to play the game—and reduce them to tears.

Ms. Bristol: If you want to make an NFL tough guy cry, pick up your pen and write.

Prof. Barry: Seriously. It's true. One of the players who reads the letter, defensive tackle Steve McMichael, you know what his nickname was on the field?

Ms. Bristol: No.

Prof. Barry: Mongo.

Ms. Bristol: Mongo?

Prof. Barry: Yeah. Mongo. Can you believe that? It comes from the name of a character in the Mel Brooks movie *Blazing Saddles*. The guy is so mean and crazy, he punches a horse. Can you imagine being assigned to block a guy a like that, a guy named Mongo? Imagine how hard you'd be trying to get one of your teammates to switch with you.

Ms. Bristol: Definitely.

Prof. Barry: Yet as big and bad as Steve "Mongo" McMichael was, he immediately transformed into a soft, almost cuddly, bundle of warmth and affection once he started reading Buddy Ryan's letter.

That's the power of writing. It's a power so strong that, as I suggested at the beginning of class, we might better think of it as a superpower—the equivalent of Superman's ability to fly, or Wolverine's ability to heal, or Wonder Woman's ability to understand and speak every human language. So internalize the following phrase, everybody. It's our version of "If you want to change the world, pick up your pen and write."

Ms. Bristol: "Writing is a superpower."

Prof. Barry: It really is. For more proof, we can take a quick tour through American history.

44

Writing Is a Superpower

Prof. Barry: Let's start with the eighteenth century. Think about the Declaration of Independence and Thomas Paine's pamphlet *Common Sense*. Think about the Constitution and the collection of essays known as *The Federalist Papers*. No offense to the Boston Tea Party and the shots fired at Lexington and Concord, but the American Revolution was, in many ways, a written revolution. New phrases, new sentences, and new documents created a new nation.

And then, in the nineteenth century, when that new nation became a divided nation as well as one increasingly crippled, morally, by the systematic enslavement of human beings, books by two unlikely heroes—Frederick Douglass and Harriett Beecher Stowe—helped do something extraordinary, even magical: correct the country's conscience.

Ms. Franzoni (*jumping in*)**:** Isn't there a story about how when Abraham Lincoln first met Harriet Beecher Stowe a couple years into the Civil War, he greeted her by saying something like, "So you are the little lady who started this great war"?

Prof. Barry: Yeah, that's the story. You're our history major, right?

Ms. Franzoni: Right.

Prof. Barry: Did you hear the story in a class here at Michigan?

Ms. Franzoni: No. I think I read about it somewhere.

Prof. Barry: Got it. I have read about the story in a bunch of places too, but unfortunately none of those places provided a whole lot of evidence showing the conversation actually happened—or at least, not in the way it is commonly retold.

Still, the impact of Stowe's *Uncle Tom's Cabin* was undeniably immense, as was the impact of a couple of superpower-type books written in the twentieth century: *The Jungle* by Upton Sinclair and *Silent Spring* by Rachel Carson. Both led, relatively quickly, to direct congressional action. In February of 1906, for example, Sinclair published *The Jungle.* By June, Congress—responding to the novel's depiction of the meatpacking industry—passed the Pure Food and Drug Act. The idea that something needs to be "FDA-approved" owes a lot to that book, as does the entire Food and Drug Agency itself.

Interestingly, though, Sinclair thought people misunderstood his novel. He wanted readers to respond, on an intellectual level, to his critique of how immigrants and other low-wage workers were being exploited by the country's major industries. But instead, readers responded, on a visceral level, to his description of how, for instance, bits of rats made it into packages of sausages. Or how grown men, having fallen into vats of boiling chemicals, were processed into and sold as lard.

Here is what Sinclair later wrote about this disconnect.

Ms. Franzoni: "I aimed for the public's heart and by accident hit it in the stomach."

Prof. Barry: Sinclair has also become a common reference point for the second book I mentioned, *Silent Spring* by Rachel Carson. What Sinclair did for food regulation, Carson did for environmental regulation, even to the point of triggering the creation of a new government agency. There is a direct line between the publication of *Silent Spring* in 1962 and the birth of the Environmental Protection Agency, or EPA, in 1972. Last time I checked, there was even a tribute to Carson on the EPA's website, as well as the following separate acknowledgment. Read it for us, please, Ms. Franzoni.

Or wait, let's have one of the science majors do it, since Carson started out as a marine biologist. Is that okay?

Ms. Franzoni: Sure.

Prof. Barry: So let's see, we've already heard from Ms. Warsaw and Mr. Carlos today, so maybe someone else. Where's Ms. Maat?

Ms. Maat: Here.

Prof. Barry: Your résumé says you're a biology major.

Ms. Maat: So far, yeah.

Prof. Barry: Are you thinking about switching majors?

Ms. Maat: No. Maybe just adding a second one.

Prof. Barry: Geez. Not exactly taking the slacker approach to college life, are you? Perhaps you'll even follow in the footsteps of Rachel Carson and transform how we think about the environment.

First, though, please read that tribute from the EPA's website I mentioned.

Ms. Maat: "The EPA today may be said without exaggeration to be the extended shadow of Rachel Carson."

Prof. Barry: Isn't that pretty cool?

Ms. Maat: Yeah.

Prof. Barry: And it's all because Carson took the time to write her arguments down and had the skill to craft them in a powerfully persuasive way.

Ms. Maat: She was a good writer?

Prof. Barry: She was a *great* writer. Which means she might also be a helpful model for you. Carson is proof that being a scientist doesn't prevent you from being a good writer. And who knows—maybe being a good writer might even help you be a better scientist, at least in the sense that you can then more effectively share your findings and ideas with others. Think of what the ability to write did for the careers of people like Stephen Jay Gould, Evelyn Fox Keller, E. O. Wilson, Lewis Thomas, Carl Sagan, Neil deGrasse Tyson—the list goes on and on. Carson had their level of linguistic dexterity. She liked to read Melville and Thoreau. She liked to read poetry. She even liked to write poetry.

Ms. Maat: Really?

Prof. Barry: Really. You know how I said the title of her book is *Silent Spring*?

Ms. Maat: Yeah.

Prof. Barry: Well, that's a reference to a couple of lines of poetry from John Keats. Here they are.

Ms. Maat: "The sedge has withered from the lake / And no birds sing."

Prof. Barry: Kind of brutal, huh—if you think of the environmental destruction implied. Sedge is a grass-like plant. Probably not a great sign that it has "withered."

Ms. Maat: Nor that "no birds sing."

Prof. Barry: Right. That's not a good sign either.

But what's so neat about the EPA tribute is the space it devotes to this literary side of Carson as well as its suggestion that the success of *Silent Spring* had a lot to do with Carson's attention to, even love of, language. Here's the tribute's closing observation. It's a description of Carson from David Brower, who was once the past president of the Sierra Club and is a longtime conservationist.

Ms. Maat: "She did her homework, she minded her English, and she cared."

Prof. Barry: I kind of like that as a recipe for success in this course: Do your homework. Mind your English. And care.

45

WISP and Making the Most of What You Have

Ms. Ida: What about the twenty-first century, Prof. Barry? Do you have any WISP examples that are a little more recent?

Prof. Barry: WISP?

Ms. Ida: Yeah. You said that "**W**riting **i**s a **s**uper **p**ower," so I thought I'd shorten that to WISP. W-I-S-P.

Prof. Barry: I am pretty sure *superpower* is one word, but other than that, I like it. I could imagine a cool Pixar movie built around a character named Wisp. She'd travel around fixing the grammar on store signs and billboards, all while writing world-changing stories, letters, and laws. Maybe she could even have a sidekick. Like an editor.

Ms. Ida: Yeah. The editor could be the person she relies on to catch all her mistakes and awkward phrasings.

Prof. Barry: That could be the sidekick's name.

Ms. Ida: What?

Prof. Barry: Catch.

Ms. Ida: Wisp and Catch?

Prof. Barry: Yeah. Or Catch and Wisp, if you like the sound of that order better. We have some time to decide.

At the moment, though, I want to get back to Ms. Ida's question about superpower-type pieces of writing from the twenty-first century. My answer is that I actually hope somebody in here will produce one. Or maybe a few of the students I get to teach over at the law school. I tell them, whenever I can, that writing is a superpower. I tell them that it can catapult their careers, that a lawyer who is good with words is a lawyer who is extremely valuable to big firms, to small public interest organizations, to every branch of the government. I tell them that they can write their way to a better job.

Ms. Ida: Do they listen?

Prof. Barry: More and more do, yeah. They realize that if they become better writers, they will certainly become better lawyers. They see the direct relationship between those two activities.

Ms. Franzoni (*jumping in*): My mom always says that.

Prof. Barry: Is your mom a lawyer?

Ms. Franzoni: Yeah.

Prof. Barry: What kind?

Ms. Franzoni: The kind who works all the time.

Prof. Barry: That doesn't really narrow it down. But you've heard her say that lawyers are essentially professional writers?

Ms. Franzoni: Yeah, she'll say it when she's working on a brief or something. She'll call herself a writer of creative nonfiction. She can't invent facts, she says. She can't make stuff up, like a novelist. But she does, every day apparently, write stories.

Prof. Barry: I sometimes use an observation by John McPhee about creative nonfiction to get a similar point across to law students. A winner of the Pulitzer Prize—and a finalist three other times—McPhee taught a creative nonfiction course at Princeton for more than thirty years. Sometimes calling creative nonfiction "the literature of fact," he defines it this way: "Creative nonfiction is not making something up but making the most of what you have." Want to try to modify that for lawyers like your mom, Ms. Franzoni?

Ms. Franzoni: "Lawyering is not making something up but making the most of what you have."

Prof. Barry: Good. And we could certainly apply that same principle to other professions. Chefs, for example, might say that cooking is not making something up but making the most of what you have. Marketers might say that marketing is not making something up but making the most of what you have. And certainly researchers could say that research is not making something up but making the most of what you have.

Which brings me to Adam Grant, one of the more ingenious social science researchers around and someone we are going to use to start to review what we have covered today, because we are coming to the end of class.

46
Adam Grant

Prof. Barry: The main thing we have been focusing on today, Ms. Bart, is this idea that the words you choose can change the world people see, right?

Ms. Bart: Right.

Prof. Barry: And earlier, a little before we looked at that medical malpractice case, I mentioned that Adam Grant, who teaches at the Wharton School of Business, has a great example of this kind of choice. Have you ever heard of Grant, Ms. Bart—maybe in one of your business courses?

Ms. Bart: I think so, yeah. Is he the guy who wrote *Give and Take*?

Prof. Barry: He is—and he actually grew up here in Michigan.

Ms. Bart: Really? Where?

Prof. Barry: West Bloomfield.

Ms. Bart: Cool.

Prof. Barry: He also went to graduate school here.

Ms. Bart: At Michigan? He's a Wolverine?

Prof. Barry: Yeah. And so is his mom, apparently. He has said in interviews that he grew up bleeding Maize and Blue.

Ms. Bart: Did he get an MBA from here?

Prof. Barry: No. He got a PhD in organizational psychology. It took him just three short years.

Ms. Bart: That sounds fast.

Prof. Barry: It is. A lot of people take between five and seven years. Some take as long as ten.

Ms. Bart: That's what I thought.

Prof. Barry: Here are some other impressive facts about him. He has been, at various points, a Junior Olympic diver, a professional magician, the youngest tenured professor at Wharton, and Sheryl Sandberg's coauthor.

Ms. Bart: The COO of Facebook?

Prof. Barry: Yeah.

Ms. Amos (*jumping in*): Isn't he also supposed to be a super nice guy?

Prof. Barry: You've heard of Grant too, Ms. Amos?

Ms. Amos: Yeah. We read a magazine profile of him in one of my psychology classes.

Prof. Barry: From the *New York Times*?

Ms. Amos: Yup. It said that "helpfulness was Grant's credo."

Prof. Barry: Not "Greed is good"?

Ms. Amos: No. More like "Giving is good."

Prof. Barry: Well, in the example we are going to look at, he certainly helped give a whole bunch of doctors something important.

Ms. Amos: What?

Prof. Barry: A better incentive to wash their hands.

47
Clean Hands

Prof. Barry: The example comes from Adam Grant's second book, *Originals*. In it, he describes an experiment he and another psychologist, David Hoffman, conducted in a hospital. They were trying to encourage nurses and doctors to wash their hands more. Here's the first sign Grant and Hoffman posted near soap dispensers. Would you mind reading it for us, please, Mr. Carlos? Maybe their experiment is something you'll remember when you become a doctor someday.

Mr. Carlos: "Hand hygiene prevents you from catching diseases."

Prof. Barry: Now read the second sign.

Mr. Carlos: "Hand hygiene prevents patients from catching diseases."

Prof. Barry: One of these signs had no effect on handwashing. The other sign, however, led nurses and doctors to wash their hands 10 percent more often and use 45 percent more soap.

So here's the question: Which sign was it? Which one convinced the nurses and doctors, some of the busiest people around, to spend more time in front of a soap dispenser, to take an extra step toward preventing the spread of diseases?

Mr. Carlos: I'm tempted to say the first sign.

Prof. Barry: The sign that read, "Hand hygiene prevents you from catching diseases"?

Mr. Carlos: Yeah.

Prof. Barry: Why?

Mr. Carlos: Because often the best way to motivate people is to appeal to their self-interest.

Prof. Barry: And so if you are a nurse or doctor and you see that a particular action protects you from catching diseases, protects you from being harmed . . .

Mr. Carlos: You're going to take that action. You're going to wash your hands.

Prof. Barry: Exactly. But here's the thing: that's not what actually happened in the study. The sign that read, "Hand hygiene prevents you from catching diseases," the sign that appealed to people's self-interest . . .

Mr. Carlos: Yeah?

Prof. Barry: That didn't trigger more handwashing.

Mr. Carlos: But the other one did?

Prof. Barry: Yeah. The one that read, "Hand hygiene prevents patients from catching diseases." You want to try to explain why? What might account for the "you" sign triggering less handwashing than the "patients" sign?

Mr. Carlos: Is it because when nurses and doctors are prompted to focus on themselves, to imagine something bad happening to them personally, they don't weigh the risk as heavily?

Prof. Barry: Perhaps, yeah. Maybe they think, "Look, I'm around germs all day every day. I don't always wash my hands. And I'm usually fine. So I'll be fine again this time, even if I skimp a little on the Purell."

Mr. Carlos: Right.

Prof. Barry: Maybe they are, in other words, overconfident about their own invulnerability to harm?

Mr. Carlos: I think we probably all are.

Prof. Barry: I use that phrase "overconfident about their own invulnerability to harm" because it's the phrase Grant uses in *Originals*. Here's his account of why the "you" sign wasn't as effective as the "patients" sign. Read it for us, please. It's very similar to what you just said.

Mr. Carlos: "Thinking about oneself invokes the logic of consequence: Will I get sick?"

Prof. Barry: Keep going.

Mr. Carlos: "Doctors and nurses can answer swiftly with a no: I spend a lot of time in a hospital. I don't always wash, and I rarely get sick, so this probably won't affect me."

Prof. Barry: And finally, concluding with that "overconfident" phrase I mentioned?

Mr. Carlos: "In general, we tend to be overconfident about our own invulnerability to harm."

Prof. Barry: Grant suggests that the thought process is different, though, with the "patients" sign. He says that thinking about patients prompts not a "logic of consequence" but a "logic of appropriateness." When that happens, the key question becomes the following.

Mr. Carlos: "What should a person like me do in a situation like this?"

Prof. Barry: Grant clarifies what he means.

Mr. Carlos: "[The 'patients' sign] changes the calculation from a cost-benefit equation to a contemplation of values, of right and wrong. I have a professional and moral obligation to care for patients."

Prof. Barry: Pretty interesting, huh?

Mr. Carlos: Very.

Prof. Barry: You can learn more about the logic of consequence and the logic of appropriateness in the "Rebel with a Cause" section of *Originals* as well as in the research of Samuel and Pearl Oliner. Grant spends a decent amount of time on a book those two wrote called *The Altruistic Personality: Rescuers of Jews in Nazi Europe*. It asks the following question: What led ordinary men and women to risk their lives on behalf of others during the Holocaust?

But even if you don't buy into Grant's distinction between the idea of a logic of consequence and a logic of appropriateness, even if you think something else might explain why the "patients" sign was more effective than the "you" sign, the important point for us as we continue to try to understand and use more effective language is that a single word can make all the difference. As Grant and his coauthor wrote in the *Psychological Science* article where they first published their findings, "Results showed that changing a single word in messages motivated meaningful changes in behavior."

48

The Infinite Power of Grammar

Prof. Barry: There is one more concept I want to cover today. It's related to what we have been talking about—but with a slight twist. Instead of focusing on how the words you choose can change the world people see, it focuses on how the *order* of the words you choose can change the world people see.

To show you what I mean, let's look at an essay called "Why I Write" by Joan Didion, who is the author of a number of highly acclaimed books, including *The Year of Magical Thinking, Slouching towards Bethlehem,* and *The White Album.*

Anybody want to help read the slides? Maybe someone who hasn't spoken yet?

Ms. Nina: I can.

Prof. Barry: Great, thank you. It's Ms. Nina, right?

Ms. Nina: Right.

Prof. Barry: And you're a music major?

Ms. Nina: Yup.

Prof. Barry: Great. Part of what the essay highlights is the role sound should play in our writing, so you'll be perfect. Here's the opening of the passage.

Ms. Nina: "All I know about grammar is its infinite power. To shift the structure of a sentence alters the meaning of that sentence, as definitely and inflexibly as the position of a camera alters the meaning of the object photographed."

Prof. Barry: Keep reading.

Ms. Nina: "Many people know about camera angles now, but not so many know about sentences."

Prof. Barry: One more.

Ms. Nina: "The arrangement of the words matters."

Prof. Barry: There is, conveniently, a term for this idea that "the arrangement of the words matters." Any chance you know it, Ms. Nina?

Ms. Nina: Diction?

Prof. Barry: No. That's the term for word choice. We're talking about word order.

Ms. Nina: Prosody?

Prof. Barry: That's not quite it either. The term is *syntax*. When people talk about *syntax*, they are generally talking about word order, about the organization of the phrases and sentences being written or said. It's a fundamental component of communication.

Which is why this course is called what?

Ms. Nina: The <u>Syntax</u> of Sports.

Prof. Barry: And also why that other course I teach is called?

Ms. Nina: The Syntax of Slavery.

Prof. Barry: Right. My hope is that putting *syntax* in the title will help you all remember how important a factor it is to consider when writing. Shifting the structure of a sentence really can, as Didion says, alter the meaning of the sentence. Suppose, for example, you go on a date, Ms. Nina.

Ms. Nina: What kind of date?

Prof. Barry: A first date. You're nervous, you're trying to read the other person, you're not quite sure whether it will lead to anything. And then, toward the end of the date, the other person looks at you and says one of two things. Here's the first option.

Ms. Nina: "I am really interested in you, but I am also really busy this semester."

Prof. Barry: And here's the second.

Ms. Nina: "I am really busy this semester, but I am also really interested in you."

Prof. Barry: Which would you rather hear?

Ms. Nina: Do I like the person?

Prof. Barry: Yeah. A lot.

Ms. Nina: Then the second one, the one where my date says, "I am really busy this semester, but I am also really interested in you."

Prof. Barry: Why?

Ms. Nina: Because the last thing my date says is that they are interested in me.

Prof. Barry: Doesn't your date say that in the first example too, right at the beginning of the sentence?

Ms. Nina: Yeah, but then they say "I am also really busy this semester." As if being busy is the point they want to stress.

Prof. Barry: And by stress, you mean that's the part your date wants to make the focus, the part they want to highlight, the part that carries the most important information?

Ms. Nina: Yeah.

Prof. Barry: But you're saying it's different in the example where your date ends with "I am also really interested in you"?

Ms. Nina: Yeah. There, the focus switches. In that one, my date really seems to like me.

Prof. Barry: And presumably wants to see you again?

Ms. Nina: Right.

Prof. Barry: But when your date ends with "I am also really busy this semester"?

Ms. Nina: I feel rejected.

Prof. Barry: Even though "I am really interested in you, but I am also really busy this semester" and "I am really busy this semester, but I am also really interested in you" are, in many ways, the same statements.

Ms. Nina: Right.

Prof. Barry: They would be written using the same marks of punctuation: a comma and a period.

Ms. Nina: Right.

Prof. Barry: They use the same number of words: fourteen in "I am really interested in you, but I am also really busy this semester" and fourteen in "I am really busy this semester, but I am also really interested in you."

Ms. Nina: Right.

Prof. Barry: They even use the same exact words.

Ms. Nina: Right.

Prof. Barry: So what's the difference?

Ms. Nina: The difference is the order of the words.

Prof. Barry: So the difference is syntax?

Ms. Nina: Yeah.

Prof. Barry: Good. That's often an overlooked difference, so I want to make sure everyone in here is able to recognize the major effects it can have. Sometimes those effects are playful. One example is how the writer Steven Pressfield refashioned the title of Sun Tzu's famous book on military strategy, *The Art of War*, into something better suited for Pressfield's own book on creative strategy: *The War of Art*.

Or check out this slogan used by the magazine the *Economist* to flatter and attract readers. It rearranges the common saying "Great minds think alike."

Ms. Nina: "Great minds like a think."

Prof. Barry: Pretty good, huh?

Ms. Nina: Yeah.

Prof. Barry: Other times, though, the effects of syntax can be more consequential. Suppose, Ms. Nina, that you are representing a woman convicted of a crime. We'll call her Ms. Hester.

Ms. Nina: Okay.

Prof. Barry: And also suppose that when it comes time to sentence this woman, the judge in the case frames her decision in one of two ways. Here's option one.

Ms. Nina: "Look, I think you are genuinely sorry for the harm you have caused, and I also think you are committed to becoming a productive member of society—but the crime you committed warrants a significant punishment."

Prof. Barry: And here's option two.

Ms. Nina: "Look, the crime you committed warrants a significant punishment—but I think you are genuinely sorry for the harm you have caused, and I also think you are committed to becoming a productive member of society."

Prof. Barry: Which option do you think Ms. Hester would rather hear?

Ms. Nina: The second one.

Prof. Barry: Why?

Ms. Nina: Because of the syntax, especially the placement of the word *but.*

Prof. Barry: The placement changes the meaning?

Ms. Nina: Yeah.

Prof. Barry: So when *but* comes after the judge says Ms. Hester's crime "warrants a significant punishment"?

Ms. Nina: It sounds like Ms. Hester might catch a break.

Prof. Barry: And when *but* comes before the judge says Ms. Hester's crime "warrants a significant punishment"?

Ms. Nina: That break disappears.

Prof. Barry: Which means?

Ms. Nina: Ms. Hester is probably going to jail.

Prof. Barry: Exactly.

49

James Joyce

Prof. Barry: Examples like the one Ms. Nina just helped us explore show why writers spend so much time thinking about syntax. The best ones are not content to merely come up with the right words. They also work hard to put those words in the right order. Anybody remember the Samuel Taylor Coleridge line from the beginning of class, the one where he was defining poetry?

Mr. Dewey (*jumping in*)**:** "The best words in their best order"?

Prof. Barry: Good. "The best words in their best order." Notice Coleridge doesn't simply say "The best words." That's not enough. You also have to put them in their best order.

Mr. Dewey: Right.

Prof. Barry: Another way to understand this is through a fun anecdote about the legendary Irish writer James Joyce. You ever read anything by him, Mr. Dewey?

Mr. Dewey: Yeah. I tried reading *Ulysses* last spring.

Prof. Barry: On your own or in a class?

Mr. Dewey: On my own.

Prof. Barry: That can be dangerous.

Mr. Dewey: It certainly can. I didn't make it past the first chapter.

Prof. Barry: Yeah, that chapter is a doozy.

Mr. Dewey: Have you read the book?

Prof. Barry: I have—a few times, actually. But always with the help of a really good teacher. The world's best books, I've found, are often like the world's best cities: to get the most out of them, to move beyond just a superficial, touristy experience, it really helps to have an expert guide show you around. You need someone who is knowledgeable, someone who is patient, someone who can help you process all that you are about to encounter. Otherwise, you'll just feel lost and may never want to visit again.

Mr. Dewey: I definitely had that feeling with *Ulysses*.

Prof. Barry: You could have used a guide?

Mr. Dewey: Yeah. A whole team of them.

50
Hieroglyphics

Prof. Barry: The less-than-satisfying experience you had reading James Joyce is not uncommon, Mr. Dewey. Virginia Woolf, for example, had, at best, some pretty mixed feelings about the novel. After reading the first two hundred pages, she told a friend, "Never did I read such tosh." She also called it the work of "a queasy undergraduate scratching his pimples."

Mr. Dewey: I'm guessing Joyce didn't use that as a book blurb?

Prof. Barry: Nope. Nor did he use anything from his wife, Nora Barnacle, who didn't even make it to page 200. She gave up at page 27.

Mr. Dewey: Really?

Prof. Barry: Yup. She joked with Joyce that perhaps one day he might write a book people could understand.

Other people, of course, have been much more admiring. Ernest Hemingway described *Ulysses* as "a most god-damn wonderful book"; T. S. Eliot credited Joyce with producing a book "to which we are all indebted, and from which none can escape"; and the Modern Library, a collection of influential literary types, named *Ulysses* the best English-language novel of the twentieth century—and it gave third-place honors to another of Joyce's efforts.

Mr. Dewey: *Dubliners?*

Prof. Barry: *Dubliners* is a collection of short stories, not a novel.

Mr. Dewey: *Finnegans Wake?*

Prof. Barry: Nope. *A Portrait of the Artist as a Young Man.*

Mr. Dewey: So where did *Finnegans Wake* rank? Isn't that another of his famous ones?

Prof. Barry: *Finnegans Wake* didn't even make the list. People seem to consider it more an experiment than a novel.

Ms. Yona (*jumping in*): One of the requirements for my major—

Prof. Barry: Comparative literature, right?

Ms. Yona: Yeah. Comparative literature. One of the requirements for it is that we have to take courses on books written in a foreign language. And a friend of mine, a native English speaker, joked that *Finnegans Wake* should count as one of those foreign-language books.

Prof. Barry: Because it's so incomprehensible?

Ms. Yona: Yeah.

Prof. Barry: That's funny, and not exactly unwarranted. *Finnegans Wake* is a pretty wild book. On the first page of the novel appears something like the following. I'll see if I can write it on the board.

> *"Bababdaldharaghuakmmiaronnkonrontnnrrontonbthlnnrovr roinansawntoohoooordennthurnnk!"*

Mr. Dewey: Seriously?

Prof. Barry: I'm probably off by a few letters—but yeah, go to the library and see for yourself. You'll think you've discovered a new form of hieroglyphics.

51

Neil Gaiman, Mark Twain, and Wiel Coerver

Prof. Barry: As difficult as *Finnegans Wake* is at times, there are also some really beautiful sentences in it. Here's one, although you are going to have to ignore that Joyce writes the conjunction "and" in some funky ways: first as "und," then as "ant," and finally as "end."

Mr. Dewey: "They lived und laughed ant loved end left."

Prof. Barry: Even with the funkiness, doesn't that construction have a nice rhythm to it?

Mr. Dewey: Yeah.

Prof. Barry: It's also a good example of alliteration and polysyndeton.

Mr. Dewey: What's polysyndeton?

Prof. Barry: It's when writers intentionally add to a sentence a bunch of coordinating conjunctions—which are words like *and, or, nor*—for stylistic effect. For example, Joyce could have written that sentence in the standard way, separating the first three verbs with commas: "They lived, laughed, loved, and left." But instead he added in extra conjunctions, albeit deliberately misspelled: "They lived und laughed ant loved end left."

Mr. Carroll (*jumping in*): Like the Big Bad Wolf.

Prof. Barry: Exactly. Like the Big Bad Wolf. In *The Three Little Pigs*, the Big Bad Wolf doesn't say, "I'll huff, I'll puff, and I'll blow your house in!" Instead, he says?

Mr. Carroll: "I'll huff and I'll puff and I'll blow your house in!"

Prof. Barry: When we replace the commas with conjunctions, the words now build off one another a bit more kinetically. It's a pretty cool writerly move.

Mr. Carroll: Rough name, though.

Prof. Barry: Polysyndeton?

Mr. Carroll: Yeah.

Prof. Barry: I know. It sounds like a chemical compound. Or something you might use to insulate your attic.

Which is why we're going to call it something different, something that honors a writer who uses polysyndeton often and well.

Mr. Carroll: Who?

Prof. Barry: Neil Gaiman.

Mr. Carroll: The science fiction writer?

Prof. Barry: Gaiman does write science fiction. But he also writes children's stories and screenplays and a whole bunch of other stuff—which is partly why he's such a good ambassador for polysyndeton: he, just like the polysyndeton move itself, generously grabs in and embraces so much of the world and its imaginative possibilities. Check out, for example, the New Year's greeting he first posted back in 2001.

Mr. Carroll: "May your coming year be filled with magic and dreams and good madness."

Prof. Barry: Keep reading.

Mr. Carroll: "I hope you read some fine books and kiss someone who thinks you're wonderful."

Prof. Barry: And now read what the wish says after offering the following reminder: "Don't forget to make some art."

Mr. Carroll: "Write or draw or build or sing or live as only you can."

Prof. Barry: Notice how the conjunction Gaiman uses this time is *or*, not *and*. I encourage you to experiment with each of them when trying out polysyndeton. The same goes for *nor*. They can all create the grabbing effect Gaiman uses so well.

Mr. Carroll: Maybe that's what we should call the move instead of "polysyndeton." We should call it "the Grab of Gaiman."

Prof. Barry: Close. Just reverse the order and get rid of the *of*.

Mr. Carroll: "The Gaiman Grab"?

Prof. Barry: Yup. Over the years, I've found that students remember and use polysyndeton a lot more when they don't have to remember that it's called polysyndeton, when they can simply think of it as a Gaiman Grab, a name directly associated with a writer they know and admire. We're going to do that a lot, actually.

Mr. Carroll: Name writing moves?

Prof. Barry: Yeah. And sometimes even link them to really good writers. It's sort of what the legendary Dutch soccer coach Wiel Coerver did with dribbling moves. Anybody ever hear of him? Maybe you, Ms. Bristol? You're our soccer player.

Ms. Bristol: I didn't know Coerver was an actual guy, but I definitely practiced all the Coerver moves growing up. It's how I learned to play.

Prof. Barry: But you never learned anything about Coerver himself.

Ms. Bristol: The person? No.

Prof. Barry: You just remember the moves?

Ms. Bristol: Yeah.

Prof. Barry: Okay. So I'll fill you in a little bit. Coerver was, as I said, Dutch, and in the 1970s, he developed a very systematic, almost academic, approach to teaching soccer skills. He watched footage of the best players in the world—Pelé, Beckenbauer, Bobby Charlton. He broke their playing down into discrete moves. And then he had his own players practice those moves over and over again, all with the idea that greatness can be taught, that the brilliant movements on display can be learned, that skill and creativity are not necessarily innate. It was a pretty revolutionary approach.

Ms. Bristol: I totally remember doing those moves. There was "the Matthews."

Prof. Barry: Right. That move is named after the English forward Sir Stanley Matthews, the so-called Wizard of the Dribble. Though perhaps he should have also been called the "Wizard of Longevity." Matthews played, professionally, all the way until the age of fifty.

Ms. Bristol: Another one I remember was "the Rivellino."

Prof. Barry: Yup. That was named after Roberto Rivellino. He played midfield on what many consider the greatest soccer squad ever assembled: the 1970 Brazilian World Cup team. He also rocked one of the greatest mustaches ever assembled.

Ms. Bristol: Yeah. I really liked the Rivellino. It was one of the first moves I learned.

Prof. Barry: Is it your favorite?

Ms. Bristol: No.

Prof. Barry: What is?

Ms. Bristol: "The Cruyff."

Prof. Barry: Oh, yeah, that's a good one.

Ms. Bristol: I know.

Prof. Barry: You want to try to describe it for us?

Ms. Bristol: I don't know if I can.

Prof. Barry: Yeah, describing soccer moves is tough. It's sort of like what is sometimes said about trying to describe music, especially in writing: "Writing about music is like dancing about architecture."

But give it your best shot.

Ms. Bristol: Okay. Say you're dribbling in one direction.

Prof. Barry: Right.

Ms. Bristol: What the Cruyff allows you to do is use your feet to tuck the ball behind your opposite heel so you can then dribble in the opposite direction.

Prof. Barry: And you really like that move?

Ms. Bristol: Yeah. I use it pretty much every time I play.

Prof. Barry: Was it helpful, when you were learning the move, to know that it had a name?

Ms. Bristol: Very.

Prof. Barry: Why?

Ms. Bristol: I don't know. I guess saying "the Cruyff" is just a lot shorter than saying "the turn where you tuck the ball behind your opposite heel so you can change direction." Plus, it's also more precise.

Prof. Barry: More precise?

Ms. Bristol: I think so, yeah.

Prof. Barry: In what sense?

Ms. Bristol: In the sense that "the Cruyff" is a specific term rather than an elaborate description. Once you learn the mechanics of the move—where your hips go, where the ball will be, where the defender is likely to end up—hearing "the Cruyff" triggers something very particular in your mind.

Prof. Barry: And in your feet, let's hope.

Ms. Bristol: Right.

Prof. Barry: You think something similar happens with figure skaters when they hear "a Double Axel"?

Ms. Bristol: Probably.

Prof. Barry: How about high jumpers when they hear "the Fosbury Flop"?

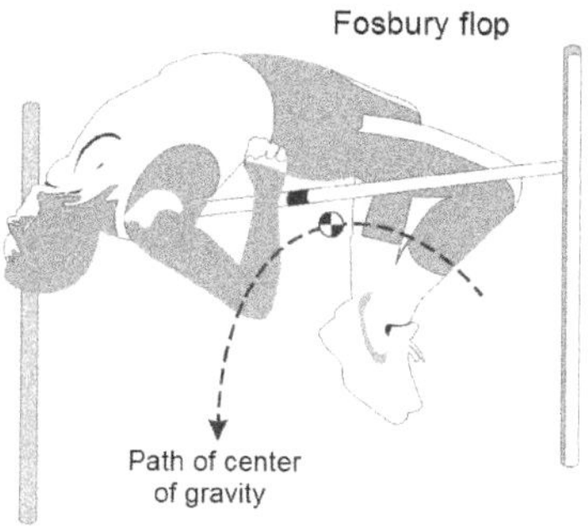

Ms. Bristol: Yeah.

Prof. Barry: Or even every day, in the morning, when people are getting dressed and hear, in their head, while tying their tie, "the Windsor Knot."

Ms. Bristol: Definitely. It's just a lot easier to learn and remember something when it has a name.

Prof. Barry: I couldn't have said that any better myself.

52

To Name Is to Know and Remember

Prof. Barry: We can find support for the point you just made, Ms. Bristol, in the book *The Future of Life* by the biologist E. O. Wilson. Explaining that the beginning of every science is the description of phenomena, Wilson writes the following about the value of naming things.

Ms. Bristol: "We cannot think clearly about a plant or animal until we have a name for it; hence the pleasure of bird-watching with a field guide in hand."

Prof. Barry: We can also find support for it in a book by the philosopher Susanne Langer, who has spent a lot of time thinking about symbols and art and language—and actually taught here at Michigan for a little while. Here are the lofty terms she uses to describe the power of naming things.

Ms. Bristol: "The notion of giving something a name is the vastest generative idea that ever was conceived."

Prof. Barry: But my favorite comment on naming—particularly the kind of naming we'll be using in this class, the kind that activates learning and memory—comes from Dana Gioia, a poet that Ms. Bart might actually get a kick out of.

Ms. Bart: Why?

Prof. Barry: Because he claims to be the only person ever to go to business school to become a poet.

Ms. Bart: He went to business school?

Prof. Barry: Yeah. He earned his MBA from Stanford and then, for years, worked as an executive at the food giant General Foods. He spent a decent amount of time marketing the Kool-Aid brand and was also part of the team that invented "Jell-O Jigglers."

Ms. Bart: I guess that explains the alliteration.

Prof. Barry: Maybe. Gioia is pretty darn good with words. That's actually the name of the poem we're going to look at.

Ms. Bart: "Good with Words"?

Prof. Barry: Nope. It's even simpler than that: the title is just "Words." Would you mind reading the beginning for us?

Ms. Bart: "The world does not need words. It articulates itself / in sunlight, leaves, and shadows. The stones on the path / are no less real for lying uncatalogued and uncounted."

Prof. Barry: Isn't that pretty cool? Gioia is essentially asking, "Look, who needs these silly abstractions called 'words'?"—especially when all around us is a much more natural form of communication: sunlight, leaves, shadows, the stones on the path he mentions.

Plus, it's not as if those stones, or any other phenomena, are desperately waiting for us to classify and measure them. Their existence does not depend on any label or name. As Gioia explains in the very next line, "The fluent leaves speak only the dialect of pure being."

Ms. Bart: That kind of sounds like something you might see above the door of a yoga studio. "In here, we speak only the dialect of pure being."

Prof. Barry: Fair enough. But the point Gioia is making is worth considering and might make us reevaluate the importance we have been placing, during today's entire class, on words.

Perhaps we actually overvalue words. Perhaps they are not as important as we think. The poem is even about to suggest that words can often take something wonderful—like a kiss—and corrupt it, turning it into "something less or other."

Read the section where this suggestion appears. I'll give you the lead-in line: "The kiss is still fully a kiss even though no words were spoken."

Ms. Bart: "And one word transforms it into something less or other— / *illicit, chaste, perfunctory, conjugal, covert.*"

Prof. Barry: See? Before, "the kiss" was just a kiss. But now, because of these modifying words, it's an "illicit kiss" or a "perfunctory kiss" or a "covert kiss." With those additions, it's been sullied.

Ms. Bart: So words are bad?

Prof. Barry: No. Word's aren't bad, necessarily. But sometimes they can tarnish what they touch. And sometimes they're just plain inadequate. One of my own favorite teachers, James Boyd White, once wrote a book that examined, very skillfully, this general idea. Here's the title.

Ms. Bart: *When Words Lose Their Meaning*.

Prof. Barry: Yet what is so great about Gioia's poem, at least for our purposes, is that at the same time that it acknowledges the limits of words, it also celebrates, in a later stanza, their pedagogical power.

Read that stanza for us, please. It ends with an observation that motivates a lot of what we will be doing in this class: "To name is to know and remember."

Ms. Bart:

> *Yet the stones remain less real to those who cannot*
> *name them, or read the mute syllables graven in silica.*
> *To see a red stone is less than seeing it as jasper—*
> *metamorphic quartz, cousin to the flint the Kiowa*
> *carved as arrowheads. To name is to know and remember.*

Prof. Barry: Writing-move by writing-move, we are going to develop a vocabulary each of you can use to both *identify* effective writing and *produce* effective writing. Just as "stones remain less real to those who cannot name them," so too do powerful forms of expression remain less real—and less attainable—to those who cannot name them.

So get ready to spot, and then try out for yourself, a little "O-balance" and "Touch of Twain." Prepare next class for a lesson on "the Power of the Particular" and, after that, one on "the Rule of Three."

We even make time for "Rhetorical Repetition" and "the Nifty Not."

Ms. Bart: The Nifty Not?

Prof. Barry: Yeah. A lot of the names we learn will be a little silly, like the Nifty Not. Some aren't even my own. But all are pretty helpful, or at least they have been with past students. Years after taking the course, many tell me they still remember these names. Even better, they tell me they continue to use the moves to improve how they communicate. And of course, if you don't like the names we come up with, there are usually more formal alternatives.

Ms. Bart: Like polysyndeton?

Prof. Barry: Yeah, like polysyndeton—or its linguistic pal, "asyndeton." There are whole books filled with technical terms like these. But I figured we'd try to come up with some of our own. The English language could use some better marketing.

53
Positive No

Prof. Barry: We are closing in on the last minutes of class. But before you go today, I want to give you one more example of how a subtle shift in language can lead to a larger shift in perspective.

I want to give it to you because I know many of you are still trying to figure out your schedule for the semester—and frankly, figuring out your schedule is something you are going to have to do, often with much bigger consequences, for the rest of your life. What commitments should I say yes to? What commitments should I say no to? How do I achieve that elusive thing called work-life balance?

Ms. Bart: When do we have to decide whether this class is a commitment we are going to say yes to?

Prof. Barry: Usually the registrar's office gives about three weeks. So I guess after our second or third class?

Ms. Henrietta: We're only meeting once a week?

Prof. Barry: Yeah. I intentionally scheduled our first class to be a slightly longer session because I knew we had a bunch of introductory material to cover. But the rest of the time, we'll meet for only about ninety minutes. It's not the ideal way to teach writing. But given my other responsibilities—

Ms. Bart: At the law school?

Prof. Barry: Yeah, at the law school. Given those, we have a limited set of options. Which is kind of what this final example of shift in language is about.

Ms. Bart: Limited options?

Prof. Barry: Well, maybe more like choosing between options. It comes from the book *The Power of a Positive No* by William Ury, who teaches negotiations at Harvard Law School. Maybe you've heard of one of his previous books, *Getting to Yes*. He cowrote that with Roger Fisher in 1981, and it has since sold millions of copies.

Ms. Bart: Sounds somewhat familiar.

Prof. Barry: Check it out sometime. It's really popular among business folks. For now, though, let's focus on *The Power of a Positive No* because its key insight provides a nice cap to the emphasis we've been placing on how the words you choose can change the world people see. You want to read that insight for us, please?

Ms. Bart: "Every No is a Yes someplace else."

Prof. Barry: What Ury encourages people to do is essentially reframe the act of saying no to an unwanted obligation as saying yes to yourself and what is important to you. Here's one way he explains it.

Ms. Bart: "Only by saying No to competing demands for your time and energy can you create space for the Yeses in your life, the people and activities that really matter the most to you."

Prof. Barry: That might sound a little self-help-y, but it remains an important lesson. College is only the beginning of a large phase of your life where you are going to have to make some hard choices about how to spend your time. You're going to feel bad about saying no to things. You're going to think you're missing out on stuff, that you're letting people down.

Ury himself claims to feel this all the time. A highly sought-after teacher, negotiator, and writer, he constantly has to turn down requests to lead an executive education course, or mediate a conflict, or contribute to a book. And that's just in his professional life. Imagine how many dinner invitations he's probably declined over the years, how many trips to the movies he's skipped, how many afternoons with his kids he's cut short. Like the rest of us, he just doesn't have time to do everything he'd like.

Ms. Bart: Sometimes it feels like I don't even have time to think about how I don't have time.

Prof. Barry: What seems to have helped Ury, and maybe something we should all try as well, is to remember that every time you say no to one thing, you are giving yourself the chance to say yes to something else.

In Ury's case, saying no to leading an executive education course might mean getting to say yes to a little more time with his son on the Abraham Path, a long-distance walking trail he helped set up in the Middle East. Or saying no to a dinner invitation might mean getting to say yes to an article in *National Geographic* he's been meaning to read. He has a PhD in anthropology, after all.

Ms. Bart: Really? He's an anthropologist?

Prof. Barry: Yeah. A surprising number of business thinkers are. But even if our own time trade-offs aren't as attractive-sounding as Ury's, we can all think of a day, I hope, when saying no to an afternoon workout, or happy hour, or trip to the grocery store might mean getting to say yes to one of the most glorious activities of all.

Ms. Bart: What?

Prof. Barry: A nap.

Ms. Bart: If I get to say yes to a nap, Prof. Barry, I will say no to anything you want.

Prof. Barry: Including me?

Ms. Bart: What do you mean?

Prof. Barry: Borrowing from Ury, I'm making one of the requirements for this course a "Positive No." At some point during the semester, you need to say no to an assignment I ask you to do. Or even say no to showing up for a particular day of class.

Ms. Bart: You want us to skip class?

Prof. Barry: It's not really skipping if you tell me ahead of time—which is part of the requirement. You can't just *not* show up one day. I want you to tell me, at least a few days in advance, "Prof. Barry, I am not coming to class. I am doing something else instead." And then I want you to say what that something else is.

Ms. Bart: Seriously?

Prof. Barry: Seriously. But let me reiterate: saying what you'll be doing instead of coming to class is one of the most important parts of the requirement. We are not doing this so that you can practice saying no indiscriminately. I am not teaching you to be a flake.

We are doing this so you can practice saying no with purpose, with forethought, with a targeted sense of what, by saying no, you can then say yes to.

Ms. Bart: Do you always do this with your classes?

Prof. Barry: The more recent ones, yeah.

Ms. Bart: Even at the law school?

Prof. Barry: Especially at the law school. It's one of my favorite assignments.

Ms. Bart: Why?

Prof. Barry: Because I think the ability to say no to things, to realize that your time and energy are not inexhaustible resources, is one of the more important skills you can learn as you enter adulthood, particularly once you start to enjoy a little success, as I hope all of you will.

Remember Neil Gaiman, the writer we named that polysyndeton move after?

Ms. Bart: Yeah.

Prof. Barry: Well, he said some really thoughtful things about this balance during a commencement speech in Philadelphia back in 2012. He specifically addressed what he called the "problems of success."

Read a little bit of it for us, please.

Ms. Bart: "The problems of success. They're real, and with luck you'll experience them. The point where you stop saying yes to everything, because now the bottles you threw in the ocean are all coming back, and [you] have to learn to say no."

Prof. Barry: Keep reading.

Ms. Bart: "I watched my peers, and my friends, and the ones who were older than me and [saw] how miserable some of them were: I'd listen to them telling me that they couldn't envisage a world where they did what they had always wanted to do anymore, because now they had to earn a certain amount every month just to keep where they were."

Prof. Barry: A little more.

Ms. Bart: "They couldn't go and do the things that mattered, [the things] that they had really wanted to do; and that seemed as big a tragedy as any problem of failure."

Prof. Barry: He then says that the biggest problem of success is the accompanying distractions. For Gaiman, that meant a frustrating shift away from the thing that made him successful in the first place: writing stories.

Here's how he puts it.

Ms. Bart: "There was a day when I looked up and realized that I had become someone who professionally replied to email, and who wrote as a hobby."

Prof. Barry: So he made a "Positive No"-type change.

Ms. Bart: "I started answering fewer emails and was relieved to find I was writing much more."

Prof. Barry: See? Every no is a yes someplace else. You say no to replying to some emails, or at least replying to them in an unnecessarily involved way, and you free up time to say yes to an activity that is much more meaningful to you. In Gaiman's case, the more meaningful activity was writing stories. For all of you, it can be any number of things—school-related, not school-related, whatever. It can even be replying to emails, the very thing Gaiman was trying to cut back on, if that is a meaningful activity to you.

Ms. Bart: What have past students picked for their Positive No?

Prof. Barry: All kinds of stuff. One student used her Positive No to make time to call her mom and have an unrushed conversation, something she said she hadn't been doing enough that semester. Another student used it to more thoroughly prepare for an Organic Chemistry exam. She had her sights set on medical school.

Ms. Bart: You can use it to spend time on another class?

Prof. Barry: You can use it to spend time on pretty much anything you want. I just want to make sure you make that choice deliberately. One of my favorite examples was a Thursday back in 2014 when a student used his Positive No to watch the first full day of college basketball during March Madness. He was a senior at the time, and he told me he was going to be pretty bummed to miss class, especially because we were going to talk about an essay by his favorite sports writer, Bill Simmons.

But this student had apparently always wanted to watch those opening Thursday games live, start to finish, without any interruptions from school or work. So he decided to take full advantage of the opportunity.

Ms. Bart: Was it worth it?

Prof. Barry: Definitely. That Thursday turned out to be one of the more exciting Thursdays in March Madness history. North Dakota State upset Oklahoma. Harvard upset Cincinnati. And Texas needed a last-second lay-up to hold off Arizona State. Plus, Michigan played that day.

Ms. Bart: Did we win?

Prof. Barry: Yeah. But even if we hadn't, or even if that Thursday turned out to be one of the most boring Thursdays in March Madness history, the student's choice would still have been, I think, the right one. He thought hard about how to use his Positive No. He didn't waste it in on a meaningless afternoon. Nor was he naïve about the opportunity cost of his choice. He missed a good class. And he knew he was going to miss a good class. Yet he also knew that if he came to it, he'd miss something much more special, at least to him, on that day. It's tough to think of a better use of the Positive No than that.

54

Only as Good as Your Writing

Prof. Barry: We only have a few moments left, so I want to close where, in some ways, we began: with a headline.

Would you mind reading it for us, please, Ms. Bart? It appeared in the *Harvard Business Review* in 2013.

Ms. Bart: "Your Company Is Only as Good as Your Writing."

Prof. Barry: Kind of a bold statement, right?

Ms. Bart: Yeah.

Prof. Barry: But also maybe kind of true, if we really think about how much of what a company does depends on carefully crafted written words—its marketing campaigns, its branding efforts, its ventures into social media.

Ms. Bart: Right.

Prof. Barry: And that doesn't even count things like contracts, letters to shareholders, instructional manuals, and of course, emails. If your employees can't email—if the directions they send out are unclear, if the tone they adopt is inappropriate—you're going to have a lot of headaches as a manager.

And it's not just in the business world where the importance of writing is key—we could reimagine the *Harvard Business Review* headline in many different ways. Here's one.

Ms. Bart: "Your Law Firm Is Only as Good as Your Writing."

Prof. Barry: Here's another.

Ms. Bart: "Your Non-Profit Is Only as Good as Your Writing."

Prof. Barry: Even in a field like math, which we often think is composed more in symbols than in sentences, the ability to communicate effectively, the ability to explain things in a fresh and elegant way, can really set you apart.

Case in point: Freeman Dyson, a world-renowned mathematician and physicist who spent much of his career at the Advanced Institute of Study at Princeton.

Ms. Warsaw (*jumping in*)**:** Isn't that where Albert Einstein worked?

Prof. Barry: Yeah, for about twenty years. Same with J. Robert Oppenheimer, a key figure in the development of atomic energy. Same with George Kennan, a key figure in the development of American foreign policy. And same with John von Neumann, a key figure in too many fields to mention. Freeman Dyson's forty-plus-year tenure at the Advanced Institute of Study overlapped with all those brains.

Which is pretty good for a guy who claimed that he has just two skills: doing mathematical calculations and—any guesses what the second is?

Ms. Warsaw: Are you going to say "writing"?

Prof. Barry: Yup. He said being a good writer was a tremendous way to broaden his audience and advance his career. He also said it brought him a lot of joy, especially when a book or article of his inspires someone he's never even met to write to him with a response. All this is why, as he explained in an essay for the National Writing Project in 2012, "I advise young people to exercise their writing skills as much as possible."

And now that our first class is coming to an end, I am going to tell you all something similar: before you graduate, please, *please* take some writing classes. They don't have to be with me. They don't have to be this semester. But at some point, and with a really good set of teachers, definitely take some writing classes. Make sure you get to write something every week. Make sure you get feedback every week. And then, once you do eventually graduate and head out into the wider world, make sure you don't let your writing skills atrophy. Or in the words of the poet Jane Kenyon, who was actually born here in Ann Arbor and then went on to attend both college and graduate school at Michigan, "Be a good steward of your gift."

The advice comes from notes to a lecture Kenyon gave at a literary conference in 1991. Would you mind reading a little bit more of it for us, Ms. Warsaw?

Ms. Warsaw: Sure.

Prof. Barry: Although aimed at poets, it seems like it could apply to people engaged in all kinds of creative undertakings.

Ms. Warsaw: "Protect your time. Feed your inner life. Avoid too much noise. Read good books, have good sentences in your ears. Be by yourself as often as you can. Walk. Take the phone off the hook. Work regular hours."

Prof. Barry: So with that bit of wisdom, I'm going to let you all go. Have a nice rest of the—

Mr. Dewey (*jumping in*): Wait!

Prof. Barry: Yes?

Mr. Dewey: You didn't tell us the anecdote about James Joyce, the one involving syntax.

Prof. Barry: I know.

Mr. Dewey: You know?

Prof. Barry: Yeah. I'm leaving that for our second class.

Mr. Dewey: Why?

Prof. Barry: So that you all have an incentive to come back.

Notes

Chapter 3

7 **"twelve seconds"** *Outback Bowl*, ESPN, Jan. 1, 2013, http://www.espn.com/college-football/playbyplay?gameId=330010130.

Chapter 4

11 **"Bitter Ending"** *South Carolina 33, Michigan 28: Gamecocks' Big-Play Capabilities Produce a Bitter Ending for Wolverines' Season*, DETROIT FREE PRESS, Jan. 2, 2013.

Chapter 5

14 **"one of my own teachers"** The teacher is the wonderful James Boyd White, from whom I took two courses as a graduate student.

Chapter 6

17 **"Thrilling"** Darryl Slater, *South Carolina Beats Michigan 33-28 in Thrilling Outback Bowl*, POST & COURIER, Jan. 1, 2013.

Chapter 7

19 **"he studied what you're studying"** For an account of Kahneman's time in college and graduate school, *see* Michael Lewis, THE UNDOING PROJECT: A FRIENDSHIP THAT CHANGED OUR MINDS (2016).

21 **"final-day deficit"** Christopher Clarey, *Home Is Where the Heartbreak Is*, N.Y. TIMES, Sept. 30, 2012, https://www.nytimes.com/2012/10/01/sports/golf/europe-rallies-for-stunning-victory-at-ryder-cup.html (explaining that this game was "the most remarkable comeback or collapse in the 85-year history of the Ryder Cup"). For an in-depth look at the 2012 Ryder Cup, at least from the perspective of Team Europe, *see* Oliver Holt, MIRACLE AT MEDINAH: EUROPE'S AMAZING RYDER CUP COMEBACK (2012).

22 **"Who's to Blame for the Meltdown?"** Cindy Boren, *Ryder Cup: Who's to Blame for the Meltdown?*, WASH. POST, Oct. 1, 2012, https://www.washingtonpost.com/news/early-lead/wp/2012/10/01/ryder-cup-whos-to-blame-for-the-medinah-meltdown/.

23 **"Europe Seal Ryder Cup"** Richard Williams, *Europe Seal Ryder Cup Win with Comeback of Epic Proportions*, GUARDIAN, Sept. 1, 2012, https://www.theguardian.com/sport/2012/oct/01/ryder-cup-europe-win-medinah.

24 **"survival rates or mortality rates"** Amos Tversky & Daniel Kahneman, *Rational Choice and the Framing of Decisions*, 59 J. Bus. S254, S254–55 (1986).

24 **"Bonuses or penalties"** *See id.* at S261. ("It is easier to forgo a discount than to accept a surcharge because the same price difference is valued as a gain in the former case and as a loss in the latter. Indeed, the credit card lobby is said to insist that any price difference between cash and card purchases should be labeled a cash discount rather than a credit surcharge.")

24 **"opportunity in every difficulty"** Winston Churchill, CHURCHILL BY HIMSELF: THE DEFINITIVE COLLECTION OF QUOTATIONS 577 (Richard Langworth ed., 2011).

24 **"inconvenience rightly considered"** G. K. Chesterton, ALL THINGS CONSIDERED 36 (1908).

Chapter 8

26 **"Italy won. France lost"** Daniel Kahneman, THINKING, FAST AND SLOW 363 (2011).

Chapter 9

31 **"You don't win silver"** Lisa Leslie, *Nike–You Don't Win Silver, You Lose Gold*, YOUTUBE, Oct. 14, 2012, https://www.youtube.com/watch?v=ZnLCeXMHzBs.

Chapter 10

34 **"championship game"** For a player's account of Michigan's wild run to the championship game, *see* Josh Bartelstein, WE ON: AN INSIDE LOOK AT MICHIGAN'S FINAL FOUR RUN (2015).

34 **"Louisville"** For details on Louisville's championships season, *see* The Louisville Cardinal, UNBREAKABLE: LOUISVILLE'S INSPIRED 2013 CHAMPIONSHIP RUN (2013).

35 **"Hail, Hail"** Shawn Windsor, *Hail, Hail to the NCAA Runner-Up*, DETROIT FREE PRESS, Apr. 10, 2013.

Chapter 11

39 **"six weeks it took me to get into this dress"** MovieAwardsAll, *Golden Globes 2013 Opening–Tina Fey and Amy Poehler*, YOUTUBE, 5:02–5:11, Jan. 14, 2013, https://www.youtube.com/watch?v=F4rSKCXqEw0.

Chapter 12

42 **"great documentary"** HARVARD BEATS YALE 29–29 (Kevin Rafferty Productions, 2008).

43 **"'You play football, am I right?'"** Manohla Dargis, *Back in 1968, When a Tie Was No Tie*, N.Y. Times, Nov. 18, 2008, https://www.nytimes.com/2008/11/19/movies/19harv.html.

Chapter 18

57 **"Harvard Beats Yale, 29–29"** The comma doesn't appear in the title of the documentary, but it does appear in the original headline.

Chapter 20

63 **"'the best words in their best order'"** Samuel Taylor Coleridge, Table Talk of Samuel Coleridge: And the Rime of the Ancient Mariner, Christabel, etc. 63 (1894).

63 **"'Poetry and Meaning'"** Howard Nemerov, *Poetry and Meaning*, 22/23 Salmungundi 42 (1973).

Chapter 21

66 **"braiding your hair"** Edwidge Danticat, Krik? Krak! 220 (1995).

66 **"so many broken shards"** Rafael Campo, *Of Poetry and Medicine: Rafael Campo in Conversation*, Poets.org, Mar. 1, 2006, https://www.poets.org/poetsorg/text/poetry-and-medicine-rafael-campo-conversation.

67 **"live and bear fruit"** Oliver Wendell Holmes, *Oration before the Harvard Law School Association: The Use of Law Schools* (Nov. 5, 1886), 34 Alb. L.J. 461, 461 (1886).

67 **"Order Out of Chaos"** Frank Lloyd Wright: A Film by Ken Burns and Lynn Novick, part 1 (PBS television broadcast Jan. 23, 1998); David Grann, The Devil and Sherlock Holmes 3 (2010) ("Part of the appeal of Sherlock Holmes is that he restores order to a bewildering universe."); *see also* John Lahr, *The Sphinx Next Door*, New Yorker, Sept. 21, 2015, https://www.newyorker.com/magazine/2015/09/21/the-sphinx-next-door-profiles-john-lahr ("We impose narrative on everything in order to understand it. Otherwise, there's nothing but chaos."); Steve Coll, Private Empire: ExxonMobil and American Power 35 (2012) ("'Bringing order to chaos' was the way Rockefeller had once described his monopoly."); David Wagoner, Good Morning and Good Night 45 (2005) ("A poet is trying to make music / out of the tumult of the dictionary.") (quoting Boris Pasternak); Verlyn Klinkenborg, *The Trouble with Intentions*, N.Y. Times: Opinionator, Sept. 24, 2012, https://opinionator.blogs.nytimes.com/2012/09/24/the-trouble-with-intentions/ ("Experienced writers know that every good sentence is retrieved by will from the forces of chaos."); Joan Didion: The Center Will Not Hold, 1:30 (Netflix 2017) ("It would be necessary for me to come to terms with disorder.").

68 **"Rita Dove defines poetry"** David Streitfeld, *Laureate for a New Age*, Wash. Post, May 19, 1993, https://www.washingtonpost.com/archive/politics/1993/

05/19/laureate-for-a-new-age/66ef2e1f-5bee-4025-aed9-18285afa2702/?utm_term=.5b7ddd223353 (quoting Rita Dove).

68 **"Auden suggests"** W. H. Auden et al., POETS AT WORK: ESSAYS BASED ON THE MODERN POETRY COLLECTION AT THE LOCKWOOD MEMORIAL LIBRARY 179 (1948).

Chapter 23

71 **"called Ivan Turgenev"** Patrick Waddington, TURGENEV AND GEORGE SAND: AN IMPROBABLE ENTENTE 53 (1981).

71 **"letter-writing relationship"** FLAUBERT AND TURGENEV: A FRIENDSHIP IN LETTERS; THE COMPLETE CORRESPONDENCE (Barbara Beaumont ed. & trans., 1985).

Chapter 24

75 **"Twain wasn't a fan."** Mark Twain, *Fenimore Cooper's Literary Offenses*, MARK TWAIN IN HIS TIMES (1895), http://twain.lib.virginia.edu/projects/rissetto/offense.html.

75 **"Cooper has scored 114 offenses"** *Id.*

76 **"lightning bug and the lightning"** THE ART OF AUTHORSHIP: LITERARY REMINISCENCES, METHODS OF WORK, AND ADVICE TO YOUNG BEGINNERS 87–88 (1891)

Chapter 25

77 **"Bobby Knight"** There are many books on Coach Bob Knight, some written by Knight himself. Here are few places to start: Steve Alford, PLAYING FOR KNIGHT (1989); John Feinstein, A SEASON ON THE BRINK (1986); Bob Knight & Bob Hammel, KNIGHT: MY STORY (2002); Bob Knight & Bob Hammel, THE POWER OF NEGATIVE THINKING (2013).

Chapter 26

82 **"According to Mike Davis"** Joe Drape, *College Basketball: Knight, Under Fire, Denies Manhandling Student*, N.Y. TIMES, Sept. 9, 2000, https://www.nytimes.com/2000/09/09/sports/college-basketball-knight-under-fire-denies-manhandling-student.html.

Chapter 27

87 **"Clemente's plaque"** *Clemente's Plaque Corrected*, N.Y. TIMES, Sept. 20, 2000, https://www.nytimes.com/2000/09/20/sports/clementeacutes-plaque-corrected.html.

89 **"Send Clemente"** For details on Clemente's life and playing career, *see* David Maraniss, CLEMENTE: THE PASSION AND GRACE OF BASEBALL'S LAST HERO (2006).

Chapter 28

92 **"clip on YouTube"** MrBuccos, *Roberto Clemente's 3,000th Hit*, YOUTUBE, Nov. 16, 2009, https://www.youtube.com/watch?v=XsmqqPxb_xM.

94 **"a jewel"** AMERICAN EXPERIENCE: ROBERTO CLEMENTE (PBS television broadcast June 15, 2009).

95 **"something for my mother and father in Spanish"** *1971 Pittsburgh Pirates World Series Locker Room Celebration*, YOUTUBE, July 11, 2013, https://www.youtube.com/watch?v=sVf13pJ_TqE.

Chapter 30

101 **"Turner's strategic naming tactic"** Chip Heath & Dan Heath, SWITCH 75 (2010).

Chapter 31

105 **"looking for shortcuts"** *Hank Aaron on Perseverance*, ACAD. ACHIEVEMENT, http://www.achievement.org/video/hank-aaron-interview-question-8/.

105 **"Stephen King"** Stephen King, ON WRITING (2000).

105 **"Philip Roth"** Philip Roth, EVERYMAN (2006).

106 **"Inspiration is for amateurs."** *Chuck Close Reflects on His Predilection, His Sudden Paralysis, and the Challenges of Adjusting His Work to His Physical Abilities*, CHARLIE ROSE, 14:40 (broadcast Mar. 13, 2007), https://charlierose.com/videos/19680.

Chapter 32

108 **"Being a professional"** Clyde Haberman, *David Halberstam, 73, Reporter and Author, Dies*, N.Y. TIMES, Apr. 24, 2007, https://www.nytimes.com/2007/04/24/arts/24halberstam.html.

109 **"wastepaper basket"** Peter Elbow, WRITING WITHOUT TEACHERS 8 (1973).

109 **"the right words"** *Id.* at 5.

109 **"getting water to keep flowing"** *Id.* at 28.

Chapter 33

112 **"lie down until that feeling goes away"** This quote is often attributed to Robert Maynard Hutchins, who was president of the University of Chicago from 1929 to 1945. It seems to come from an interview in a 1938 magazine profile, but the structure of the sentence does not make it clear whether the author has paraphrased Hutchins or someone Hutchins referenced during the interview. *See* J. P. McEvoy, *Garlands for the Living*, AM. MERCURY, Dec. 1938, at 482, 482 ("The secret of my abundant health is that whenever the impulse to exercise comes over me, I lie down until it passes away."); *see also* Ralph Keyes, THE QUOTE VERIFIER: WHO SAID WHAT, WHERE, AND WHEN 59 (2007).

112 **"Amos Alonzo Stagg"** Amos Alonzo Stagg, UNIV. CHICAGO: ATHLETICS & RECREATION, https://athletics.uchicago.edu/about/history/amos-alonzo-stagg, last visited Mar. 16, 2019.

112 **"All American literature comes from one book"** Ernest Hemingway, GREEN HILLS OF AFRICA 17 (1935).

113 **"All football comes from Stagg"** Amos Alonzo Stagg, UNIV. CHICAGO: ATHLETICS & RECREATION, https://athletics.uchicago.edu/about/history/amos-alonzo-stagg, last visited Mar. 16, 2019.

114 **"Naismith and his peach baskets"** Bob Rains & Helen Carpenter, JAMES NAISMITH: THE MAN WHO INVENTED BASKETBALL 29–31 (2009).

Chapter 34

116 **"Grab a pillow"** Jhumpa Lahiri, THE NAMESAKE 16 (2003).

Chapter 35

118 **"separated by a common language"** *Britain and America Are Two Nations Divided by a Common Language*, QUOTE INVESTIGATOR, Apr. 3, 2016, https://quoteinvestigator.com/2016/04/03/common/.

118 **"The Canterville Ghost"** Oscar Wilde, *The Canterville Ghost*, *in* LORD ARTHUR SAVILE'S CRIME & OTHER STORIES 90, 94 (1891).

Chapter 37

128 **"just an extra"** A CALL TO AMERICA: INSPIRING QUOTATIONS FROM THE PRESIDENTS OF THE UNITED STATES 97 (Bryan Curtis ed., 2002).

128 **"every exit as an entrance"** Tom Stoppard, ROSENCRANTZ AND GUILDENSTERN ARE DEAD act 1 (1966).

129 **"depending on your perspective"** Colson Whitehead, SAG HARBOR 118 (2009).

129 **"holes tied together with string"** Julian Barnes, FLAUBERT'S PARROT 38 (1984).

Chapter 38

132 **"A patient"** J. M. Williams & Gregory G. Colomb, STYLE: TOWARD CLARITY AND GRACE 65 (1990).

Chapter 39

137 **"'listen to one another'"** Verlyn Klinkenborg, SEVERAL SHORT SENTENCES ABOUT WRITING 35 (2012).

Chapter 40

141 **"20,000 lice left"** Heinrich Himmler, speech at meeting of SS commanders in Kharkow, Apr. 24, 1943 (transcript available at Library of Congress, Nazi Conspiracy and Aggression, vol. IV, 574), https://www.loc.gov/rr/frd/Military_Law/pdf/NT_Nazi_Vol-IV.pdf.

Chapter 41

144 **"Michael King Day"** DeNeen L. Brown, *The Story of How Michael King Jr. Became Martin Luther King Jr.*, WASH. POST: RETROPOLIS, Jan. 15, 2019, https://www.washingtonpost.com/history/2019/01/15/story-how-michael-king-jr-became-martin-luther-king-jr/?utm_term=.82421c3c2db3.

Chapter 42

146 **"Stanford's Carol Dweck"** Carol Dweck, MINDSET: THE NEW PSYCHOLOGY OF SUCCESS (2006).

146 **"diffidence that faltered"** Ezra Pound, SELECTED CANTOS OF EZRA POUND 85 (1988).

147 **"the shortstop's dream"** Chad Harbach, THE ART OF FIELDING 99 (2011).

147 **"the creature you were in the beginning"** Samuel Beckett, MOLLOY 32 (1951).

147 **"nudge the world a little bit"** Tom Stoppard, THE REAL THING act 2 (1982).

148 **"you can change it"** John Romano, *James Baldwin Writing and Talking*, N.Y. TIMES, Sept. 13, 1979, https://www.nytimes.com/1979/09/23/archives/james-baldwin-writing-and-talking-baldwin-baldwin-authors-query.html. The examples can certainly continue. President Theodore Roosevelt once talked about how "words are my instruments." *The Roosevelts: A Film by Ken Burns* (PBS television broadcast Sept. 14, 2014). Friedrich Nietzsche claimed that "all I need is a sheet of paper; and something to write with, and then; I can turn the whole world upside down." Blago Kirov, FRIEDRICH NIETZSCHE: QUOTES AND FACTS 4 (2016). John Updike noted that writing is a "magical act" that defies "the usual earthbound laws whereby human beings make themselves known to one another." John Updike, ODD JOBS: ESSAYS AND CRITICISMS 917 (1991). And finally, there are these lines from Lord Byron's epic poem *Don Juan*:

> *But words are things, and a small drop of ink*
> *Falling like dew, upon a thought, produces*
> *That which makes thousands, perhaps millions, think*

Chapter 43

149 **"the *30 for 30* documentary"** *The 1985 Chicago Bears* (ESPN broadcast Feb. 4, 2016).

Chapter 44

155 **"Food and Drug agency"** Lauren Coodley, UPTON SINCLAIR: CALIFORNIA SOCIALIST, CELEBRITY INTELLECTUAL 45 (2013).

156 **"hit it in the stomach"** *Id.* at 46.

157 **"extended shadow of Rachel Carson"** Jack Lewis, *The Birth of EPA*, EPA, Nov. 2015, https://archive.epa.gov/epa/aboutepa/birth-epa.html.

158 **"no birds sing"** John Keats, *La Belle Dame sans Merci: A Ballad*, POETRY FOUND (1819), https://www.poetryfoundation.org/poems/44475/la-belle-dame-sans-merci-a-ballad, last visited Mar. 17, 2019.

Chapter 45

161 **"making the most of what you have"** John McPhee, *Omission*, NEW YORKER, Sept. 7, 2015, https://www.newyorker.com/magazine/2015/09/14/omission.

Chapter 46

162 **"bleeding Maize and Blue"** Dan Shaw, *Adam Grant*, MICH. ALUMNUS (Spring 2016), http://alumnus.alumni.umich.edu/adam-grant/.

163 **"Grant's credo"** Susan Dominus, *Is Giving the Secret to Getting Ahead?*, N.Y. TIMES, Mar. 27, 2013, https://www.nytimes.com/2013/03/31/magazine/is-giving-the-secret-to-getting-ahead.html.

Chapter 47

166 **"invulnerability to harm"** Adam Grant, ORIGINALS: HOW NON-CONFORMISTS MOVE THE WORLD 166 (2016).

167 **"changing a single word"** Adam M. Grant & David A. Hoffman, *It's Not All about Me: Motivating Hand Hygiene among Health Care Professionals by Focusing on Patients*, 22 PSYCHOL. SCI. 1494, 1494 (2011).

Chapter 48

169 **"position of a camera"** Joan Didion, *Why I Write*, N.Y. TIMES, Dec. 5, 1976, https://www.nytimes.com/1976/12/05/archives/why-i-write-why-i-write.html.

172 **"Great minds like a think"** *Great Minds Like a Think*, ECONOMIST, https://shop.economist.com/products/great-minds-like-a-think, last visited Mar. 17, 2019.

Chapter 50

176 **"such tosh"** James Heffernan, *Woolf's Reading of James Joyce's Ulysses, 1922–1941*, MODERNISM LAB, https://modernism.coursepress.yale.edu/woolfs-reading-of-joyces-ulysses-1922-1941/, last visited Mar. 17, 2019.

176 **"god-damn wonderful book"** THE LETTERS OF ERNEST HEMINGWAY: VOLUME I, 1907–1922 (Sandra Spanier & Robert W. Trogdon ed., 2011).

176 **"to which we are all indebted"** T. S. Eliot, *Ulysses, Order, and Myth*, THE DIAL, Nov. 1923.

Chapter 51

181 **"teaching soccer skills"** Wiel Coerver, SOCCER FUNDAMENTALS FOR PLAYERS AND COACHES (1986).

181 **"age of fifty"** For Matthews's personal account of his playing career, *see* Stanley Matthews, THE WAY IT WAS: MY AUTOBIOGRAPHY (2000).

Chapter 52

184 **"field guide in hand"** Edward O. Wilson, The Future of Life xvii (2002).

184 **"vastest generative idea"** Susanne K. Langer, Philosophy in a New Key: A Study in the Symbolism of Reason, Rite, and Art 142 (1979).

Chapter 53

189 **"Yeses in your life"** William Ury, The Power of a Positive No 19 (2007).

190 **"business thinkers"** For a quick overview of the prevalence of anthropologists in the business world, *see* Robert J. Morais & Elizabeth K. Briody, *Business Is Booming for Business Anthropology*, Am. Anthropological Ass'n, Feb. 9, 2018, https://blog.americananthro.org/2018/02/09/business-is-booming-for-business-anthropology/; and Drake Baer, *Here's Why Companies Are Desperate to Hire Anthropologists*, Bus. Insider, Mar. 27, 2014, https://www.businessinsider.com/heres-why-companies-aredesperateto-hireanthropologists-2014-3.

192 **"learn to say no"** Neil Gaiman, *Keynote Address 2012*, University of the Arts, May 17, 2012, https://www.uarts.edu/neil-gaiman-keynote-address-2012.

Chapter 54

195 **"only as good as your writing"** Kyle Wiens, *Your Company Is Only as Good as Your Writing*, Harv. Bus. Rev., July 30, 2013, https://hbr.org/2013/07/your-company-is-only-as-good-a.

197 **"I advise young people"** Freeman Dyson, *Why I Write: Freeman Dyson Puts Words into Mathematics*, National Writing Project, Oct. 4, 2011, https://www.nwp.org/cs/public/print/resource/3677.

197 **"Be a good steward of your gift"** Jane Kenyon, *Everything I Know about Poetry: Notes for a Lecture*, *in* A Hundred White Daffodils 139, 141 (1999).

Photo Credits

Chapter 4

"South Carolina's Jadeveon Clowney Puts a Jarring Hit on Michigan's Vincent Smith in the Capital One Bowl." *Aiken Standard.* December 16, 2017. https://www.aikenstandard.com/clowney-will-always-be-remembered-for-the-hit/article_9cc70438-e2c5-11e7-8b03-c30692d6f001.html. Courtesy of *Aiken Standard.*

Chapter 7

Perry, Dan. "Medinah Country Club, Medinah, Illinois." *Wikimedia Commons.* September 25, 2009. https://commons.wikimedia.org/wiki/File:Medinah_Country_Club,_Medinah,_Illinois.jpg. Courtesy of Creative Commons {cc0} https://en.wikipedia.org/wiki/en:Creative_Commons and Attribution Share Alike 2.0 Generic {cc-by-2.0} https://creativecommons.org/licenses/by/2.0/deed.en.

Chapter 8

Ruddell, David. Modified by Danyele. "Italy vs France—FIFA World Cup 2006 Final Gianluigi Buffon." *Wikimedia Commons.* Last edited January 4, 2016. https://commons.wikimedia.org/wiki/File:Italy_vs_France_-_FIFA_World_Cup_2006_final_-_Gianluigi_Buffon.jpg. Courtesy of Creative Commons {cc0} https://en.wikipedia.org/wiki/en:Creative_Commons and Attribution Share Alike 2.0 Generic {cc-by-2.0} https://creativecommons.org/licenses/by/2.0/deed.en.

Chapter 9

"United States Women's National Basketball Team." *Wikimedia Commons.* August 12, 2008. https://commons.wikimedia.org/wiki/File:United_States_women%27s_national_basketball_team.jpg. Public Domain {PD-USGov} https://commons.wikimedia.org/wiki/Template:PD-USGov.

Glanzman, Adam. "Peyton Siva Hoists Louisville's NCAA Championship Trophy in 2013." *Wikimedia Commons.* April 15, 2013. https://commons.wikimedia.org/wiki/File:Peyton_Siva_hoists_Louisville%27s_NCAA_championship_trophy_in_2013.jpg. Courtesy of Creative Commons {cc0} https://en.wikipedia.org/wiki/en:Creative_Commons and Attribution Share Alike 2.0 Generic {cc-by-2.0} https://creativecommons.org/licenses/by/2.0/deed.en.

Chapter 14

Mitchell, Jack. "Meryl Streep by Jack Mitchell." *Wikimedia Commons*. Last edited March 23, 2017. https://commons.wikimedia.org/wiki/File:Meryl_Streep_by_Jack_Mitchell.jpg. Courtesy of Creative Commons {cc0} https://en.wikipedia.org/wiki/en:Creative_Commons, Attribution Share Alike International {cc-by-sa-4.0} https://creativecommons.org/licenses/by-sa/4.0/, Attribution Share Alike 3.0 Unported {cc-by-sa-3.0} https://creativecommons.org/licenses/by-sa/3.0/deed.en, Attribution Share Alike 2.5 Generic {cc-by-sa-2.5} https://creativecommons.org/licenses/by-sa/2.5/deed.en, Attribution Share Alike 2.0 Generic {cc-by-sa-2.0} https://creativecommons.org/licenses/by-sa/2.0/deed.en, and Attribution Share Alike 1.0 Generic {cc-by-sa-1.0} https://creativecommons.org/licenses/by-sa/1.0/deed.en.

"#TBT to When Actor Tommy Lee Jones Dominated on Harvard's OLINE." *Facebook*. Harvard Football. October 26, 2017. https://www.facebook.com/HarvardFootball/posts/tbt-to-when-actor-tommy-lee-jones-dominated-on-harvards-oline-gocrimson/1688535624521959/. Courtesy of the Harvard Athletic Department.

"Al Gore, Vice President of the United States, Official Portrait 1994." *Wikimedia Commons*. Last edited October 8, 2016. https://en.wikipedia.org/wiki/File:Al_Gore,_Vice_President_of_the_United_States,_official_portrait_1994.jpg. Public Domain {PD-USGov} https://commons.wikimedia.org/wiki/Template:PD-USGov.

Chapter 15

Courtesy of Harvard Athletic Department.

Chapter 18

"Tie It Up." *Harvard Alumni*. Stories. November 7, 2013. https://alumni.harvard.edu/stories/tie-it-up. Courtesy of *Harvard Crimson*.

Chapter 20

"Coleridge." *Wikimedia Commons*. Last edited August 13, 2007. https://commons.wikimedia.org/wiki/File:Coleridge.jpeg. Public Domain {PD-US-old-70-expired} https://commons.wikimedia.org/wiki/Template:PD-old-70-expired and {PD-Art} https://commons.wikimedia.org/wiki/Template:PD-Art.

Chapter 21

Shankbone, David. "Edwidge Danticat by David Shankbone." *Wikimedia Commons*. Last edited September 18, 2007. https://commons.wikimedia.org/wiki/File:Edwidge_Danticat_by_David_Shankbone.jpg. Courtesy of Creative Commons {cc0} https://en.wikipedia.org/wiki/en:Creative_Commons and Attribution Share Alike 3.0 Unported {cc-by-sa-3.0} https://creativecommons.org/licenses/by-sa/3.0/deed.en.

"Justice Oliver Wendell Holmes at Desk." *Wikimedia Commons*. National Photo Company. Last edited December 29, 2009. https://commons.wikimedia.org/wiki/File:Justice_Oliver_Wendell_Holmes_at_desk.jpg. Public Domain {PD-US-expired} https://commons.wikimedia.org/wiki/Template:PD-US-expired.

Chapter 22

"Gustave Flaubert." *Wikimedia Commons*. Last edited June 13, 2018. https://commons.wikimedia.org/wiki/File:Gustave_flaubert.jpg. Public Domain {PD-US-old-70-expired} https://commons.wikimedia.org/wiki/Template:PD-old-70-expired.

Chapter 26

"Coach Bobby Knight." N.d. Courtesy of University of Indiana Athletic Department.

Chapter 27

Greene, William C. "Willie Mays, Standing, Wearing Baseball Uniform, with Arm around Shoulders of Roy Campanella." *New York World-Telegram and Sun*. Library of Congress. Last edited May 14, 2009. Public Domain https://commons.wikimedia.org/wiki/File:Willie_Mays_cropped.jpg.

According to the library, there are no known copyright restrictions on the use of this work. This photograph is a work for hire created prior to 1968 by a staff photographer at the *New York World-Telegram and Sun*. It is part of a collection that was donated to the Library of Congress, and per the instrument of gift, it is in the public domain.

Chapter 32

Petteway, Steve. "Sonia Sotomayor in SCOTUS Robe." *Wikimedia Commons*. Last edited September 15, 2009. https://commons.wikimedia.org/wiki/File:Sonia_Sotomayor_in_SCOTUS_robe.jpg. Public Domain {PD-USGov} https://commons.wikimedia.org/wiki/Template:PD-USGov.

"Julius Ervin—76ers." *Wikimedia Commons*. Last edited February 12, 2014. https://commons.wikimedia.org/wiki/File:Julius_Erving_%E2%80%93_76ers_(1).jpeg. Public Domain {PD-US-no notice} https://commons.wikimedia.org/wiki/Template:PD-US-no_notice.

"UChicago Football Stag 1892." *Wikimedia Commons*. Last edited September 16, 2009. https://commons.wikimedia.org/wiki/File:Uchicago_football_stagg_1892.jpg. Public Domain {PD-US-expired} https://commons.wikimedia.org/wiki/Template:PD-US-expired.

Chapter 36

"Cottage Guesthouse." Aberdeen, Scotland. 2018. Photo courtesy of Barbara Stewart, the best Scottish mum an American soccer player could have.

Chapter 37

"Professor Barry and Scotti." *Press and Journal* (Aberdeen, Scotland). 2013. Courtesy of DC Thomson.

Hill, W. E. "Youngoldwoman." *Wikimedia Commons*. Last edited August 22, 2005. https://commons.wikimedia.org/wiki/File:Youngoldwoman.jpg. Public Domain {PD-US-expired} https://commons.wikimedia.org/wiki/Template:PD-US-expired.

Chapter 40

"Bundesarchiv Bild 183-R99621, Heinrich Himmler." *Wikimedia Commons*. Last edited December 20, 2018. https://commons.wikimedia.org/wiki/File:Bundesarchiv_Bild_183-R99621,_Heinrich_Himmler.jpg. Courtesy of Creative Commons {cc0} https://en.wikipedia.org/wiki/en:Creative_Commons and Attribution Share Alike 3.0 Germany {cc-by-sa-3.0-DE} https://creativecommons.org/licenses/by-sa/3.0/de/deed.en.

Chapter 41

Cranach the Eder, Lucas. "Martin Luther." *Wikimedia Commons*. Last edited June 16, 2013. https://en.wikipedia.org/wiki/File:Martin_Luther,_1529.jpg. Public Domain {PD-US-old-100-expired} https://commons.wikimedia.org/wiki/Template:PD-old-100 and {PD-Art} https://commons.wikimedia.org/wiki/Template:PD-Art.

"Martin Luther King, Jr." *New York World-Telegram and Sun*. 2004. Library of Congress.

According to the library, there are no known copyright restrictions on the use of this work. This photograph is a work for hire created prior to 1968 by a staff photographer at *New York World-Telegram and Sun*. It is part of a collection that was donated to the Library of Congress, and per the instrument of gift, it is in the public domain.

Chapter 43

Souza, Pete. "Mike Ditka Presents Jersey to Former President Barak Obama." *Obama White House*. Archives. October 7, 2011. https://obamawhitehouse.archives.gov/blog/2011/10/07/1985-chicago-bears-visit-white-house. Courtesy of *Obama White House*.

Chapter 44

Warren, George Kendall. "Fredrick Douglass (circa 1879)." *Wikimedia Commons*. Last edited August 12, 2006. https://commons.wikimedia.org/wiki/File:Frederick_Douglass_(circa_1879).jpg. Public Domain {PD-US-old-70-expired} https://commons.wikimedia.org/wiki/Template:PD-old-70-expired.

"Beecher-Stowe." *Wikimedia Commons.* Last edited October 21, 2009. https://en.wikipedia.org/wiki/File:Beecher-Stowe.jpg. Public Domain {PD-US-expired} https://commons.wikimedia.org/wiki/Template:PD-US-expired.

Chapter 49

"James Joyce by Alex Ehrenzweig, 1915." *Wikimedia Commons.* Last edited February 26, 2011. https://commons.wikimedia.org/wiki/File:James_Joyce_by_Alex_Ehrenzweig,_1915_cropped.jpg. Public Domain {PD-US-expired} https://commons.wikimedia.org/wiki/Template:PD-US-expired.

Chapter 51

"Roberto Rivelino 1974." *Wikimedia Commons.* January 18, 2013. https://commons.wikimedia.org/wiki/File:Roberto_Rivelino_1974c.jpg. Courtesy of Creative Commons {cc0} https://en.wikipedia.org/wiki/en:Creative_Commons and Attribution Share Alike 3.0 Netherlands {cc-by-sa-3.0-NL} https://creativecommons.org/licenses/by-sa/3.0/nl/deed.en.

"Stanley Matthews 1962." *Wikimedia Commons.* Last edited October 27, 2017. https://commons.wikimedia.org/wiki/File:Stanley_Matthews_1962_(crop).jpg. Courtesy of Creative Commons {cc0} https://en.wikipedia.org/wiki/en:Creative_Commons and Attribution Share Alike 3.0 Netherlands {cc-by-sa-3.0-NL} https://creativecommons.org/licenses/by-sa/3.0/nl/deed.en.

Siegrest, Alan. "Image Showing Path of Center of Gravity in Fosbury Flop." *Wikimedia Commons.* Last edited August 17, 2016. https://en.wikipedia.org/wiki/Fosbury_Flop#/media/File:Fosbury_Flop_English.gif. Courtesy of Creative Commons {cc0} https://en.wikipedia.org/wiki/en:Creative_Commons and Attribution Share Alike International {cc-by-sa-4.0} https://creativecommons.org/licenses/by-sa/4.0/.

Chapter 54

"Freeman Dyson." *Wikimedia Commons.* June 14, 2011. https://commons.wikimedia.org/wiki/File:Freeman_dyson.jpg. Courtesy of Creative Commons {cc0} https://en.wikipedia.org/wiki/en:Creative_Commons and Attribution Share Alike 3.0 Unported {cc-by-sa-3.0} https://creativecommons.org/licenses/by-sa/3.0/deed.en.